another country

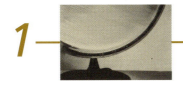

1 — The New Support Arrangements for Asylum Seekers

New national support arrangements for asylum seekers aim to fulfil the UK's international commitments while discouraging economic migration. However, dispersal will not be an easy policy to implement.

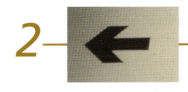

2 — Planning for Dispersal – the Role of Regional Consortia

As multi-agency partnerships, regional consortia are well-placed to develop a strategic response to dispersal. Proactive management of community relations will be vital.

3 — Providing Support Services at the Local Level

For dispersal to work, local agencies need to address gaps in services and take a lead from authorities that have developed successful, innovative projects for asylum seekers and refugees.

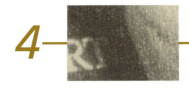

4 — Strengthening the National Framework

The efforts of local agencies will not deliver better standards of support unless there are parallel improvements in the national framework.

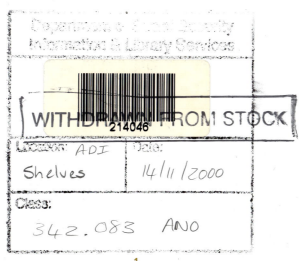

Contents

© Audit Commission 2000

First published in June 2000 by the Audit Commission for Local Authorities and the National Health Service in England and Wales, 1 Vincent Square, London SW1P 2PN

Printed in the UK for the Audit Commission by Holbrooks Printers Ltd, Portsmouth

ISBN 1 86240 224 8

Photographs: Robert Harding (pp7, 19), Pam Isherwood/Format (p45), Hilary Shedel (pp55, 69), Tony Stone (cover, p5), Telegraph Colour Library (pp3, 81)

Preface

How you are with the one to whom you owe nothing, that is a grave test and not only as an index of our tragic past. I always think that the real offenders at the halfway point of the century were the bystanders, all those people who let things happen because it didn't affect them directly. I believe that the line our society will take in this matter – on how you are to people to whom you owe nothing – is a signal.

Rabbi Hugo Gryn (Ref. 1)

As long as there is conflict there will be refugees. And as one of the first countries to sign up to the 1951 United Nations Convention Relating to the Status of Refugees, the UK has a proud history of providing sanctuary for those fleeing war or persecution. In turn, many refugees and their communities have made an enormous contribution to British society, enriching its political, economic and cultural life. Many famous exiles – such as Karl Marx, Sigmund Freud and Wole Soyinka – have lived in the UK and contributed to its multi-cultural and multi-racial identity.

However, in recent years, the growing number of asylum seekers arriving in the UK, partly as a result of increased mobility and developments in communications, has put the asylum system under severe strain. The number of people claiming asylum increased dramatically from about 4,000 a year in 1988 to over 70,000 in 1999 (Ref. 2). Largely as a result of this increase, the backlog of asylum seekers awaiting a decision, and the costs of supporting them, have increased substantially. In some cases, those who apply are fleeing poverty rather than persecution. Yet no matter how rational the desire for a prosperous life, it does not bring entitlement to refugee status. It is therefore important to have systems in place that determine swiftly, but fairly, whether a claim for asylum is genuine. In the interim, those awaiting a decision require support.

The Immigration and Asylum Act 1999 aims to address perceived weaknesses in the UK's asylum system and to 'deliver a firmer, fairer and faster approach to immigration control' (Ref. 3). New centralised support arrangements for destitute asylum seekers are one element of the new approach. These seek to fulfil the UK's international commitments, while discouraging economic migration by minimising cash payments to asylum seekers and providing only a basic level of support. Additionally, they aim to relieve pressure on London and Kent by dispersing asylum seekers to locations across Britain on a 'no-choice' basis.

Without effective support, asylum seekers could easily become locked in a cycle of exclusion and dependency in their new community.

Although these arrangements effectively 'nationalise' support for asylum seekers, local agencies still have a vital role. A wide range of support services, such as education and healthcare, will continue to be provided at a local level. For local agencies with little knowledge of the cultural needs of asylum seekers, or the problems that new arrivals often face in using services, dispersal will represent an immense challenge. Local government and its partners need to learn fast and plan well if they are to meet the needs of this vulnerable group. Failure to do so could escalate community tensions and incur substantial long-term costs. An inadequate response will also cause severe distress to asylum seekers and constrain the long-term opportunities of those allowed to stay in this country. Without effective support, asylum seekers could easily become locked in a cycle of exclusion and dependency in their new community. Alternatively, they could simply 'vote with their feet' and return to London, again putting pressure on health and education services in the capital.

The main aim of this report is to help local agencies to make the policy of dispersal work. Although written principally for local government and health authorities, some of its findings and recommendations are relevant to other partner organisations, such as housing associations, police authorities and the employment service. And areas with established asylum-seeking and refugee communities may also find the report useful – much good practice exists in these areas but it is not universal. Finally, the findings and recommendations raise issues for the Home Office and other government departments. (A briefing aimed specifically at council and health authority members and senior officers is also available.)

This study is based on visits to 15 fieldwork sites – 10 councils and 5 health authorities.[I] All of the sites visited had substantial experience of providing services to asylum seekers, either under social services legislation or as part of the recent Kosovan Humanitarian Evacuation Programme. The findings are also informed by an Audit Commission survey of all social services authorities in England and Wales,[II] and other published research.

I   Local authorities visited comprised: four London boroughs, one county council, two district councils, two metropolitan boroughs and one Welsh unitary authority. Health authorities included four based in London and one in the north west.

II A questionnaire was sent to all (171) social services authorities in England and Wales; 101 responses were received.

The study team comprised Sára Kulay, Katharine Knox and Manisha Patel from the Audit Commission's Public Services Research Directorate, with consultancy support from Sasha Acimovic, under the direction of Kate Flannery. An advisory group drawn from local government, central Government, other professional bodies and the voluntary sector, provided invaluable assistance (see Appendix 1). A refugee community panel, with representatives from a range of refugee community organisations, provided vital insights into the day-to-day experiences of asylum seekers (Appendix 2). Additional information on the Government's plans for dispersal and support for asylum seekers was provided by the National Audit Office. The Commission is grateful for all of these contributions but, as always, responsibility for the conclusions and recommendations rests with the Commission alone.

Glossary

The following terms are used throughout this report:

- **Asylum seekers** are people who flee their home country and seek refugee status in another, possibly because of war or human rights abuses. Under Part V1 of the Immigration and Asylum Act 1999, the term asylum seeker includes people who claim that their removal will breach Article 3 of the European Convention on Human Rights that prohibits torture, inhuman or degrading treatment or punishment.

- **Refugee status** – a person is recognised as a refugee when the government of the new country decides that they meet the definition of a refugee under the 1951 United Nations (UN) Convention Relating to the Status of Refugees [BOX A]. A person with refugee status is given indefinite leave to remain (ILR) in the UK.

- **Exceptional leave to remain (ELR) or exceptional leave to enter (ELE)** is granted to asylum seekers who, despite failing to meet the strict definition of a refugee, are allowed to stay in the country for a definitive period for other reasons – for example, because it would be dangerous for them to return to their home country. Those with ELR or ELE status may apply for settlement after four years.

- **Settlement** is the process by which refugees become integrated into society in their new country. When a person is granted indefinite leave to remain (ILR), this is sometimes also described as 'settlement'.

BOX A

The 1951 United Nations (UN) Convention Relating to the Status of Refugees

The UK is a signatory to the 1951 UN Convention Relating to the Status of Refugees. This requires the Government to offer refuge to a person who:

'...owing to a well-founded fear of being persecuted for reasons of race, religion, nationality, membership of a particular social group or political opinion is outside the country of his nationality and is unable, or owing to such fear, is unwilling to avail himself of the protection of that country; or who, not having a nationality and being outside the country of his former habitual residence as a result of such events, is unable or, owing to such fear, is unwilling to return to it'.

The Convention also requires signatories to make social welfare available to those who are recognised as refugees on the same basis as to its own citizens.

Source: UN Convention Relating to the Status of Refugees

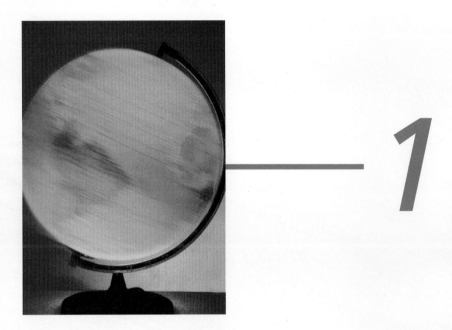

1

The New Support Arrangements for Asylum Seekers

A new national dispersal policy for destitute asylum seekers will be phased in during 2000, largely to relieve the pressure on local authorities in London and Kent. But problems encountered under previous dispersal schemes suggest that it will not be an easy approach to implement. Poor joint working, inadequate local services or lack of political support could potentially jeopardise the new arrangements.

In recent years, the asylum system has been under severe strain...

1. Displaced by continuing ethnic conflict, Mr P arrived in the UK from Rwanda at the beginning of 1999. On arrival at Gatwick he passed through immigration control because he thought that he needed a lawyer before claiming asylum. He slept on the street for three nights before finding a lawyer to help him. She took him to the Home Office in Croydon to make an application for asylum; he then went to a social services department in London to claim support. After waiting several hours, he was surprised to be told that he was being given accommodation in a place called Margate, and was issued with travel tickets and a map. He thought it was somewhere in London and was amazed to find how far it was on the train.

2. Now living in a hotel, he feels completely disorientated. There is no one who speaks his language and he is unsure of his rights. Can he go to the doctor, or enrol to learn English without any money? Concerns about his claim for asylum overshadow all other concerns about his accommodation, but he has no money to ring his solicitor. During the day he is bored; he has to leave his hotel in the morning and spends his days wandering up and down the streets. Although some of the staff at the hotel are friendly, he feels very visible and exposed in the town; people stare at him as if he is from another planet. He is very anxious for news about his missing wife and children, but without any community groups it is hard for him to get news from his country. When, after six months in the UK, he gets the right to work he intends to move back to London to be nearer to other Rwandans.

3. Ms C arrived from Kenya on the same day, after being attacked and raped in her own country. She flew directly to Heathrow and claimed asylum immediately on arrival; she spent the first night in a hotel near the airport. The Refugee Arrivals Project explained that there was no accommodation in London and put her on a coach to Birmingham. The hostel she now lives in is fine, but she doesn't know how to work the heating in her room and often feels cold. After a few days, she learnt that she is HIV positive, almost certainly contracting the disease when she was raped in Kenya. She is unsure if there is any treatment for the disease and received no further advice or support from the hospital. Sitting alone in her room, she is completely traumatised, but as one of only three women in the hostel, she feels there is nobody to whom she can turn for help.

4. These scenarios, based on real case studies documented by the Asylum Rights Campaign, reflect the experiences of many asylum seekers in the UK (Ref. 4). In recent years, the asylum system has been under severe strain, largely due to the increases in the number of new arrivals. In 1999, over 70,000 people claimed asylum in the UK, the highest level ever recorded. The Home Office has not been able to keep pace with the rising number of asylum claims and the backlog is just under 100,000 (Ref. 2), with an average wait of over a year for an initial decision (Ref. 5). Pressures at

the centre have increasingly cascaded to the local level. Following the withdrawal of social security benefits from 'in-country' applicants under the Asylum and Immigration Act 1996, many social services authorities have had to provide support for destitute asylum seekers. Most of those who need support arrive in the south east, and many councils in London and Kent are struggling to support new applicants within their areas, due largely to a shortage of affordable temporary accommodation. As a result, many have been forced to disperse asylum seekers outside London and the south east on an ad hoc basis, often to areas with no support infrastructure.

5. The Immigration and Asylum Act 1999 – the third major piece of legislation on asylum and immigration issues in the last ten years – seeks to address these problems. It includes measures that are designed to control the number of asylum seekers entering the country; to speed up the decision-making process; and to support those who have no other means of support while their application is being considered. A summary of the Act's principal measures is set out in Appendix 3.

6. The Act established a new directorate within the Home Office – the National Asylum Support Service (NASS) – to assume responsibility for supporting destitute asylum seekers and to provide them with financial support, mainly in the form of vouchers. To relieve pressure on London and Kent, NASS intends to disperse asylum seekers across Britain on a 'no choice' basis, to areas that have available accommodation, existing multi-ethnic populations and the scope to develop voluntary and community support services. The dispersal arrangements commenced on 3 April 2000 and will be phased in gradually throughout the year.

7. One objective of the Act is to minimise the incentives for economic migration. The Government's rationale for providing basic support is that this will reduce the number of people who come to the UK to escape deprivation rather than persecution, thereby minimising demands upon taxpayers. Last year, 37 per cent of asylum applicants were judged not to have a well-founded fear of persecution and had their application refused. (Ref. 2). If backlog cases are excluded,[I] the refusal rate was 54 per cent. As the decision rate has not kept pace with increases in applications **[EXHIBIT 1, overleaf]**, demands on the public purse have increased. The Government estimated that the cost to the taxpayer of supporting asylum seekers was around £475 million in 1998/99 and expected this figure to rise to £597 million in 1999/2000 (Ref. 6).

I   In 1999, 12,470 decisions were made under the backlog clearance process that granted ELR or refused cases where applicants applied prior to 1996. Of these, over 90 per cent were granted ELR.

8. It remains to be seen whether the number of new arrivals will fall under the new support arrangements. Although the number of applicants fell for a short period around the time of the introduction of the Asylum and Immigration Act 1996, there is not a simple relationship between the level of welfare benefits and the number of people who seek asylum. For example, around 60 per cent of applicants continued to claim asylum after entering the country last year even though they could not access welfare benefits (Ref. 2). And recent increases in immigration have not been confined to the UK – asylum applications to Western European countries increased by 28 per cent between 1997 and 1999 (Ref. 2). This upward trend is likely to reflect a range of social, economic and political factors, including historical patterns of settlement, improved transport and communications and political upheaval in Eastern Europe.

How will the new support arrangements work?

9. The new support arrangements represent a significant change to the previous system for supporting destitute asylum seekers, relieving local authorities of what have often been difficult responsibilities [BOX B]. Instead, NASS will assess whether new asylum seekers are eligible for support and ensure that it is provided.

EXHIBIT 1

Total number of asylum applications and decisions in the UK, 1990–99

The number of asylum applications increased significantly in 1999, but decisions have failed to keep pace.

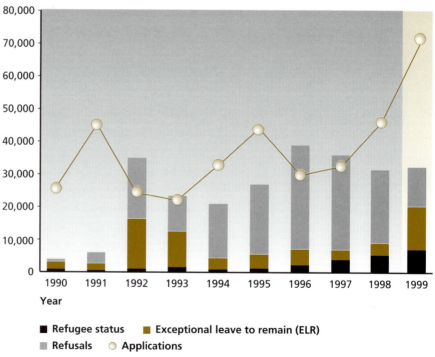

Total number of applications/decisions

- ■ Refugee status
- ■ Exceptional leave to remain (ELR)
- ■ Refusals
- ○ Applications

Source: Audit Commission based on Home Office Statistics (Ref. 2)

BOX B

Overview of previous support arrangements for asylum seekers

Under the Asylum and Immigration Act 1996, 'port of entry' asylum seekers – those who claimed asylum immediately on entry to the UK – were entitled to welfare benefits and housing, if they met 'priority need' criteria and were covered by homelessness legislation. The Act withdrew benefits from those who applied 'in-country' – those who sought asylum only after they had come into the UK – and envisaged no alternative financial provision.

Shortly after the legislation was introduced, the High Court ruled that local authorities had a duty to support single destitute asylum seekers under the National Assistance Act 1948. Because of their duties under the Children Act 1989, local authorities were also required to support asylum-seeking families on the grounds that the children could be held to be vulnerable if their parents had no means to house and feed the family. Social services authorities quickly had to set up arrangements to provide asylum seekers with housing and subsistence. As single adult asylum seekers supported under the National Assistance Act could not be provided with cash, authorities had to use alternative approaches, ranging from meals-on-wheels to food vouchers exchangeable in local supermarkets.

Interim arrangements under Schedule 9 of the Immigration and Asylum Act 1999 came into force in December 1999. These replaced local authorities' responsibilities under social services legislation with a new specific duty of support, requiring councils to support destitute in-country applicants (although a cash payment of £10 per week could now be paid to single adult asylum seekers). Under the new duty, authorities are also allowed to 'transfer' supported asylum seekers to another local authority, providing the latter agrees to take responsibility for providing support.

Authorities in London and Kent have so far supported the vast majority of those asylum seekers without access to benefits. This is largely because these areas include the major ports of arrival (Heathrow, Gatwick or Dover). In addition, as at least 85 per cent of asylum seekers and refugees are estimated to live in London (Ref. 7), the capital has gradually built up a support infrastructure that attracts incoming groups. This includes well-established voluntary and community support networks, and a range of specialist services, such as legal advice and medical treatment for victims of torture.

Source: Audit Commission

Arrival and assessment

10. The first step for port-of-entry applicants is an initial interview with an immigration officer; for those claiming asylum in-country, applications are made to the Home Office Immigration and Nationality Directorate (IND) based in Croydon. Following this interview, applicants are either granted temporary admission to the UK or taken into detention. Those granted temporary admission normally receive a standard acknowledgement letter (SAL) confirming that they have applied for asylum. These letters, which include a photograph, are often the only official documents that asylum seekers possess.

11. Prior to receiving a decision on their claim, applicants may be entitled to housing and financial support. Under the new scheme, applicants granted temporary admission are referred to a voluntary sector reception assistant, funded by NASS, who establishes whether the applicant has any other means of support and, if not, arranges emergency housing until a support application to NASS has been determined [EXHIBIT 2]. The reception assistant also helps those with no means of support to complete an application form for NASS assistance. NASS determines eligibility by taking into account the amount of money or assets at the claimant's disposal. Those deemed eligible for housing and subsistence are expected to receive an offer from NASS within seven days; those refused any form of support can appeal against the decision, but will not receive any support from public funds while doing so (Ref. 9).

Dispersal and support

...dispersal will aim to create language-based 'clusters' across the UK.

12. NASS will allocate asylum seekers to accommodation outside London and the south east. In theory, they will be housed in regions where there is already a multi-ethnic population and the scope to develop voluntary and community sector support. As far as possible, dispersal will aim to create language-based 'clusters' across the UK. In practice, the availability of accommodation is likely to be the determining factor in the final placement – the Home Office acknowledges that, if accommodation is in short supply, the other criteria will assume a lesser priority (Ref. 8).

13. Those with no other means of financial support are provided with an income set at 70 per cent of income support rates (although a child's allowance will be the same as the full rate.) Although income support rates vary according to a person's age or family size, single adult asylum seekers aged 25 or over will receive around £36 per week and couples with one child £84 per week on average. Of these sums, £10 per week per person is paid in cash and the rest in vouchers. The Government justifies providing financial support below income support rates on the grounds that the property will be furnished and utilities will be included as part of the accommodation. Additionally, as the IND aims to process claims more quickly, asylum seekers are not expected to survive on this amount for very long. The 'principal applicant' will get a book with receipts that can be exchanged for cash and vouchers weekly at a main post office; vouchers can be redeemed in a network of retail outlets.

EXHIBIT 2

The new support system for asylum seekers

New arrangements aim to ensure that key decisions about support are made within days of an asylum seeker's arrival.

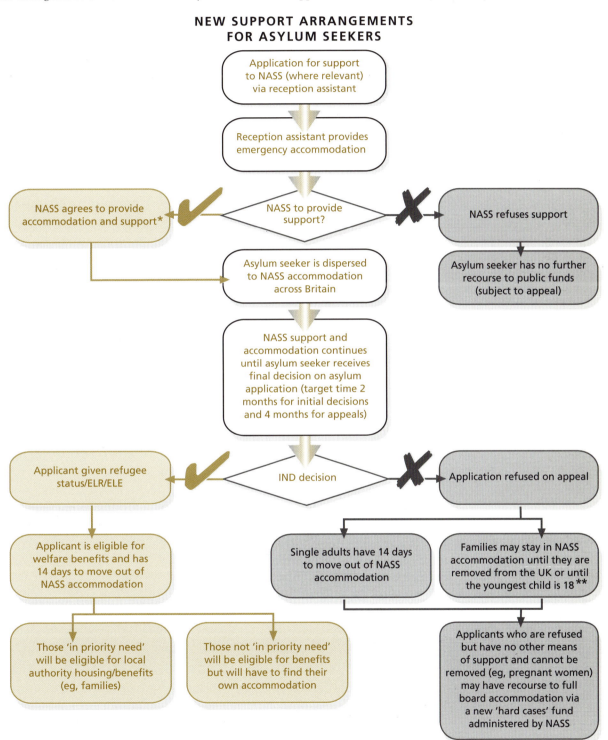

NEW SUPPORT ARRANGEMENTS FOR ASYLUM SEEKERS

Note: *NASS may provide subsistence only if an applicant can find accommodation with friends or relatives who may not be in a position to provide them with the financial resources for their other support. It may also be possible for an asylum seeker to require accommodation, but not other support, on the basis of a modest level of income that would not cover housing costs.
** NASS expects families who receive a negative decision to leave voluntarily.

Source: Audit Commission

14. Further support will be channelled through one-stop shops, established regionally and run by voluntary sector organisations such as the Refugee Council and Refugee Action. These will:

- help asylum seekers gain access to mainstream services and voluntary and community support in their area;

- develop new community support networks; and

- promote the settlement of those given refugee status or ELR.

As asylum seekers will be scattered across various cities and towns in each region, one-stop shops may have to operate on an outreach basis, possibly through drop-in sessions and surgeries.

15. Critical to the success of the Government's proposals is a significant reduction in the amount of time taken to process asylum applications. The target is that, by April 2001, first decisions will be reached within an average of two months, and any subsequent appeals will be resolved within an average of a further four months.

Termination of support

16. Asylum seekers who receive a final decision on their claim will have to move out of their accommodation in 14 days. They can seek assistance from the one-stop service on how to access housing and benefits if they are eligible. Families whose final decision is negative will be able to stay in NASS accommodation until their removal from the UK, or until their youngest child reaches 18 or they obtain means and are no longer destitute. Those asylum seekers who have their application refused but still have an outstanding claim under Article 3 of the European Convention on Human Rights (ECHR) continue to be entitled to support. From October 2000, appeals against refusal of asylum and appeals under the ECHR will be determined through a one-stop appeal process.

17. Even after a final refusal of a claim, some asylum seekers cannot be removed from the UK. This category includes pregnant women, people who are ill or those seeking a judicial review of their case. While people in these circumstances will not be entitled to any statutory provision, they may qualify for 'hard cases' provision from the Home Office. This cash-limited fund (£6 million in 2000/01) will be administered by NASS; successful applicants will be offered full-board accommodation outside London rather than cash and vouchers. At present, many people remain in the country for some time after receiving a final negative decision; between 1995 and 1999 there were 29,730 removals (including voluntary departures) while 116,155 cases (including backlog cases) were refused, although some of those refused may have decided to appeal (Ref. 2).[1] Of those who remain in the country, some fall into the categories listed above – others simply disappear from official view.

---

[1]   In 1999, 81 per cent of all substantive and third country refusals appealed.

Who will be supported under these arrangements?

18. The Government originally aimed to introduce the new support arrangements from April 2000, but problems in securing accommodation outside London and the south east led the Home Office to adopt a phased approach. From April 2000, NASS supports:

- all new *port* applicants who claim asylum in England and Wales;

- all asylum seekers who claim asylum in Northern Ireland or Scotland; and

- those placed in the Oakington reception centre in Cambridgeshire (Ref. 10).

New in-country applicants in England and Wales will be absorbed into the NASS scheme during the year. So, for the foreseeable future, applicants will continue to be supported under a variety of different arrangements [BOX C]. And, significantly, a large number of those who applied for asylum before April 2000 will continue to live in London and the south east for some time.

BOX C

Asylum seekers outside the NASS support arrangements

The NASS support arrangements commenced formally in April 2000 but many asylum seekers remain outside the NASS scheme:

Unaccompanied asylum-seeking children under 18 years of age
- All unaccompanied children will continue to be supported by local authorities under the Children Act 1989.

Port applicants who arrived before 3 April 2000
- Port-of-entry applicants who applied before 3 April 2000 will continue to be eligible for benefits until they receive a negative decision on their asylum claim. Individuals supported by an authority under homelessness legislation may be dispersed to other areas of the country, provided that the receiving authority agrees.

In-country asylum applicants in England and Wales before or after 3 April 2000
- All in-country asylum applicants will continue to be supported by local authorities under the arrangements set out in Schedule 9 of the Immigration and Asylum Act 1999 until 14 days after a final negative decision on their claim, or their phased transfer to NASS.

Source: Audit Commission, based on information from NASS

19. The complexity of the transitional arrangements, combined with the change in the start date of the new support arrangements, pose immense challenges for local agencies. Furthermore, the hidden costs involved in responding to an ever-changing national framework will have to be met locally. Several short-term issues arise:

- **commissioning accommodation** – NASS, the London Asylum Seekers Consortium (which acts as a dispersal agent for the London boroughs and Kent) and individual authorities will all be trying to secure accommodation outside London and the south east from councils, housing associations and private landlords. They risk competing for the same stock, and average rents in the private sector could rise as a result if no effective co-ordination is established;

- **staff training** – frontline staff in local agencies will need to be familiar with asylum seekers' rights and entitlements to services under different support schemes. For example, asylum seekers supported by NASS will receive automatically a certificate entitling them to help with NHS costs, such as prescriptions, dental treatment and sight tests; those who are supported by local authorities will still have to apply for help with NHS costs by completing an HC1 form.

- **exit strategies** – local authorities' proposals to wind down asylum seeker support teams, and reduce the level of contracted accommodation from April 2000, are now on hold. Plans will need to be revised as and when the timetable for the new arrangements becomes clear; and

- **financial and service planning** – although local authorities will continue to get government grants that are designed to meet the costs of supporting in-country applicants until their transfer to NASS, those that have been unable to support such asylum seekers within the grant thresholds will continue to subsidise this expenditure from their general revenue budget. Authorities are unlikely to have made provision for this in their 2000/01 budgets, since they expected this duty to be passed on to NASS from April 2000.

Learning lessons from other dispersal arrangements

20. The Immigration and Asylum Act 1999 introduced a national dispersal policy for all asylum seekers for the first time, but dispersal is not a new phenomenon. Groups of refugees accepted by the UK under international resettlement programmes, such as the Vietnamese in the 1970s and 1980s and the Bosnians in the 1990s, were also sent to designated locations across the country. The locations were, in most cases, determined by the availability of housing; settlement has sometimes been problematic, particularly where refugees have been subject to racial harassment or encountered difficulties in finding work. Many Vietnamese refugees, for example, drifted back from remote locations to major cities, such as Birmingham and London, that offered more economic opportunities and community support networks. By contrast, the policy of 'clustering' Bosnians promoted the development of new community networks and led to more successful settlement.

...the voluntary dispersal scheme for asylum seekers... demonstrated the difficulties of dispersal.

21. More recently, the voluntary dispersal scheme for asylum seekers, introduced by the Local Government Association (LGA) in December 1999 to relieve pressure on London and the south east, demonstrated the difficulties of dispersal. Multi-agency consortia, led by local authorities, were established in eight English regions (outside London), Wales and Scotland to co-ordinate arrangements for new arrivals and to identify accommodation in their area. The expectation was that around 2,600 cases would be dispersed each month up to the end of March 2000. However, while a number of local authorities responded positively, actual dispersal fell well short of the target. By mid-March 2000, the regional consortia had secured only 4,400 units of accommodation and only 1,910 cases had been dispersed, against an original target of 10,400 cases by the end of March (Ref. 11). Of these cases, 62 per cent had been sent to just two regions – Yorkshire and Humberside and the North West, both of which had experience of managing evacuees under the recent Kosovan Humanitarian Evacuation programme.

22. There are a number of reasons why the voluntary scheme struggled. Although the Home Secretary had urged the LGA to set up a voluntary dispersal scheme in November 1998, getting consortia arrangements up and running took much longer than anticipated, not least because of the number of different local agencies involved in providing support. Local authorities also faced a number of practical difficulties; organising transport between different locations and agreeing how to pay for it, proved a stumbling block. Asylum seekers arriving in London sometimes had to wait for transport, raising the question of which local authority should support them in the interim and for how long. With no way of predicting exactly how many people were coming, when they would arrive and how long they would stay, receiving local authorities could not plan ahead. Many were unclear about how many units of accommodation to bring on-stream, what level of support was required or the scale of the long-term financial implications.

23. Poor information flows between receiving and dispersing local authorities often compounded these problems. Those at the receiving end often had to provide for groups of asylum seekers without prior notice of the languages spoken. Others offered property, but then received no referrals. Inadequate needs assessment prior to dispersal meant that some asylum seekers were sent to areas that could not meet their needs for specialist services, such as mental health support – some applicants with higher levels of needs have been shunted from one local authority to another before being accepted. This has, in turn, highlighted the differing expectations of many receiving and dispersing local authorities. Areas without a history of supporting asylum seekers, and little existing infrastructure, are, understandably, reluctant to accept clients whom they cannot adequately support.

24. Regional consortia and the LGA are working hard to unravel many of these difficulties, but there is a more fundamental problem with dispersal – many asylum seekers simply do not want to leave London and will refuse support rather than be relocated. Of 921 referrals made to the London Asylum Seekers Consortium by early January, 15 per cent refused support and a further 22 per cent did not take up the offer of support outside the capital (Ref. 12). While this reduces costs to the taxpayer in the short term, it means that London boroughs will continue to bear the cost of services, such as healthcare and education, that are needed by asylum seekers who stay in the city. Refugee community organisations in London are receiving increasing demands for assistance by asylum seekers who reject dispersal, but most are already too financially constrained to help.

25. The voluntary arrangements demonstrated that dispersal, however rational an approach, will not be easy to implement. Without efficient procedures to move asylum seekers across the country, effective joint working and forward planning, or adequate support services, the problems encountered under these arrangements will persist. Local political concerns about the potential impact of dispersal could further jeopardise dispersal. In many areas, supporting asylum seekers is not a popular policy, and if the cost of support is borne, at least in part, by local taxpayers, community tensions may increase. For some local authorities, dispersal looks like a 'no-win' option, with no incentive to participate.

26. And yet, if these problems cause dispersal to fail, local agencies could pay a high price. Pressure on London and the south east will continue and will be compounded by ad hoc dispersal to inappropriate locations. As pressure mounts, the Secretary of State may have no choice but to use reserve powers to designate some housing authorities as 'asylum seeker reception zones', forcing them to accept new arrivals. This is unlikely to be beneficial to local agencies or asylum seekers.

27. For dispersal to work, the Government and local agencies need to draw lessons from previous experience. This report aims to help in this process. Chapter 2 examines the planning and co-ordinating role of regional consortia, identifying critical success factors in making the dispersal arrangements run smoothly. Chapter 3 focuses on the local services that are required to support asylum seekers, such as housing, education and healthcare, and highlights both good practice and areas of concern. Finally, Chapter 4 identifies measures that need to be adopted at the national level, and makes recommendations for improvements to the current arrangements.

2

Planning for Dispersal – the Role of Regional Consortia

To make dispersal work, regional consortia should plan strategically. The starting point is a sound understanding of asylum seekers' needs, alongside a review of existing service provision. Overcoming barriers to services and proactive management of community relations will be vital. More active involvement of local asylum seekers and refugees can also improve services – and help local agencies to avoid costly mistakes.

28. For dispersal to be successful, asylum seekers arriving in a new area will need access to a range of services that meet their support needs. The provision of shelter and subsistence to asylum seekers is necessary but not sufficient. Without adequate healthcare, education and social support at the outset, asylum seekers who receive a positive decision could experience endemic problems of unemployment, poor health and exclusion, particularly if there is also hostility towards the new arrivals from the local media and communities.

29. Rather than deal with scores of individual authorities and other agencies, the Government has promoted a regional consortium approach, in partnership with the Local Government Association (LGA), to manage dispersal at a local level [BOX D]. The approach each consortium adopts to support new arrivals will vary according to local circumstances. Variations between asylum-seeking communities and local support mechanisms mean that what works for Somalians in Sheffield will not necessarily work for Kosovans in Cardiff. Although the consortia are in their infancy, there are lessons to be drawn from the experiences of those areas with a longer history of supporting these groups and the voluntary dispersal arrangements. This suggests that there are six critical success factors to be addressed when planning for dispersal:

- establishing effective joint working arrangements;
- developing a strategic approach;
- involving members;
- proactive management of community relations;
- overcoming barriers to service delivery; and
- promoting refugee community development and involvement.

Each of these issues is examined below.

Establishing effective joint working arrangements

30. Effective joint working underpins dispersal, as a wide range of agencies play a role in providing or funding services for asylum seekers and refugees [EXHIBIT 3, overleaf]. Co-ordinating this number of partners is no mean feat – clarity about respective roles and responsibilities is essential to minimise duplication and ensure that limited resources are used to best effect. Capturing agreement in writing will help. Effective joint working is required at four levels:

- between local agencies;
- between departments within local authorities;
- between the regional consortia, local agencies and government departments; and
- across government departments.

BOX D

Regional consortia

Eight regional consortia outside London have been established in England:

- North West;
- Yorkshire and Humberside;
- West Midlands;
- East Midlands;
- North East;
- South West;
- South Central; and
- Eastern England.

There is also a consortium in Wales and one in Scotland. The London Asylum Seekers' Consortium currently disperses asylum seekers from the capital to other areas on behalf of the London boroughs. Under the new arrangements, it will mainly deal with asylum seekers with special needs who have to remain in the capital. Although most authorities are participating in one of the consortia, some have chosen to operate independently or not to participate (sometimes on the grounds that there are no current plans to disperse asylum seekers to their area). Kent will not receive asylum seekers under the new arrangements and there is no consortium covering the Kent/Sussex region. Areas of Sussex that receive asylum seekers may participate in consortia arrangements in the future.

Each consortium is expected to bring together the range of agencies involved in supporting asylum seekers at a local level, including health authorities, training and employment services, housing providers and voluntary and community groups. Housing providers within the consortia are also expected to provide around 40 per cent of the accommodation required in their area, under contract to NASS.

In 2000/01, each consortium will receive a grant of £100,000 to cover administrative costs (Ref. 13). Each one is expected to:

- develop a strategy for commissioning accommodation and monitoring its quality;
- facilitate liaison and joint working between local agencies providing support;
- promote positive media and public relations; and
- co-ordinate services for resettlement and tackle any gaps in services.

Source: Audit Commission, based on information from NASS

EXHIBIT 3

Agencies involved in meeting the needs of asylum seekers and refugees

Many local and national agencies play a role in meeting the needs of asylum seekers and refugees.

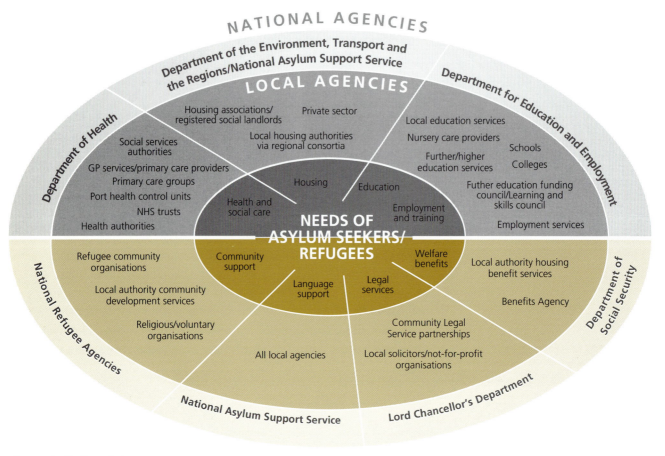

Source: Audit Commission

Inter-agency working

31. Regional consortia are to 'hold the ring' in the new support arrangements, and a number have already established joint working mechanisms [EXHIBIT 4]. Effective partnerships encompass a broad range of interests, with all players being prepared to share expertise, information and resources and to make decisions. It is also important that the key local players are involved; initially, the involvement of senior officers may be needed to persuade other stakeholders to participate, to commit their own agency to a particular course of action and to generate a clear vision of what the consortium needs to achieve. In one consortium, only local authorities are so far represented. This increases the possibility that some issues – such as the health needs of new arrivals, or the longer-term support needs of those who receive a positive decision – could be overlooked.

EXHIBIT 4

Regional consortium model being developed in the North West

Regional consortia are well placed to provide a vehicle for inter-agency working at a local level.

NORTH WEST CONSORTIUM

REGIONAL REFERENCE GROUP

MEMBERSHIP
Representatives include:
- 8 elected members and 8 local authority officers
- 2 health service representatives
- Refugee Action
- National Housing Federation
- Private sector
Membership is not fixed and could change.

ROLE
A forum for accountability, regional policy, securing co-operation and participation from members across the region.

SUB-REGIONAL TEAMS

MEMBERSHIP
Two sub-regional teams, led by Liverpool for Merseyside, Cheshire and Cumbria and Manchester for Greater Manchester. Each local authority may need its own small team for asylum seekers in its area.

ROLE
- Develop policy framework and contracting arrangements.
- Manage referrals, placements and re-housing.
- Contribute to a media strategy.

LOCAL MULTI-AGENCY GROUPS

MEMBERSHIP
At least one group per sub-region – to include:
- Statutory sector – 4 members
- Voluntary sector – 3 members
- Advice sector – 3 members
- Private sector (landlords) – 3 members
- Refugee organisations – 2 members
- Service users – 3 members
- Faith organisations – 3 members.

ROLE
Consultative and advisory, offering expertise of all sectors, overseeing work of task groups and linking with local communities.

TASK GROUPS

MEMBERSHIP
Local task groups for housing, education, adult education and training, health and social care, and advice and support linking to reception assistant.

ROLE
To address service gaps in the sub-regions and to develop services.

Note: Both London and Kent will be exporting asylum seekers under the new arrangements. Consortia boundaries may change in the future. Some parts of Sussex may accept asylum seekers under the new arrangements and participate in consortia arrangements.

Source: Audit Commission, based on information from Liverpool City Council for the North West Consortium and a map provided by the Refugee Council

Whatever structure is adopted will need to be flexible enough to cope with the changing needs of asylum seekers over time...

32. Various structural models are available, including a separate organisation with a distinct legal identity and a lead authority model where one partner – usually a local authority – contracts with NASS and manages the staff and resources for the whole region. Each has strengths and weaknesses. A separate organisation can give the partnership a strong identity and reduce the risk of domination by a single partner. But it may alienate refugee community organisations, which are not used to working in this way, while council members may fear a loss of democratic control. The lead authority model addresses these concerns but has other potential drawbacks; it may blur responsibility and accountability within the partnership and allow one or two agencies to dominate. There is no blueprint – each consortium needs to find an approach that best fits its way of working.

33. Staffing issues also require careful consideration at the outset, and will be influenced by the consortium's agreed structure. For example, most local authority asylum teams are currently managed by social services staff, yet housing and finance expertise and community development skills could be equally important in future. In practice, two-tier structures may be required; in addition to a consortium team co-ordinating region-wide activity, councils will often need their own multidisciplinary teams to manage dispersal on a day-to-day basis. Whatever structure is adopted will need to be flexible enough to cope with the changing needs of asylum seekers over time, and to respond to changes that may flow from new asylum decision-making procedures. Fast tracking some cases, for example, may rapidly lead to changes in the profile of groups being dispersed and the length of time that individuals remain in NASS accommodation.

34. While local circumstances will influence the staffing structure adopted by each consortium, the following questions are relevant to all:

- Will the structure enable the consortium to address both the strategic planning and operational tasks that it has to perform?

- Do the new arrangements build upon the expertise of existing staff?

- Can existing resources (staff and other assets) from local agencies or partnerships be pooled to support the consortium's core staffing structure?

- Are staff clear about their lines of accountability and their relationships with other bodies, such as the one-stop shops and other partner agencies?

- Is it agreed who will employ and manage the consortium's staff and other resources?

- Will the arrangements help the consortium to meet Home Office targets?

35. Regional consortia have key decisions to make, such as how resources will be managed and where asylum seekers will be accommodated within the region. Some of these decisions may provoke discord, particularly if the demand for new services exceeds the level of provision available. Differences in the values and cultural ethos of different stakeholders may also strain the partnership – some refugee community organisations may opt for a model driven by social welfare concerns, whereas housing providers' overriding objective may be simply to work within the system's financial constraints. In working through such difficulties, partnerships should tap into some existing good practice and sources of relevant information (Ref. 14).

Co-operation between departments within each local authority

36. Staff involved in the consortium should feed important messages back to departments within their authority and help to ensure that the impact of new arrangements is taken into account in service and financial planning, especially with regard to housing strategies, education development plans and children's service plans. Some plans already require agencies to set targets for this client group. For example, early year development plans for 2000/01 will need to include targets for refugee children.

37. Establishing a corporate group on asylum seekers and refugee issues within an authority can help to achieve this. The Commission's survey of social services authorities found that around one-half have already set up such a group. However, fieldwork suggests that these groups do not routinely include representatives from all key departments, or maintain awareness of relevant initiatives across the authority. In one authority, the education department was not represented; elsewhere, social services staff were unaware of funding bids being prepared by central regeneration teams that included employment and training projects for asylum seekers and refugees. In a third authority, the asylum team was unaware that the education department had produced a leaflet in seven different languages on education entitlements for asylum seekers.

Co-ordination with and between government departments

38. A number of fieldwork authorities highlighted problems caused by poor information flows between central Government and local agencies, especially with the Immigration and Nationality Directorate (IND). One authority did not receive any advance notification from the IND about plans to deport asylum seekers in its care. As a result, the authority was unaware that the council accommodation that they were occupying would be available for new cases. Failure to notify asylum seekers or local housing benefit offices of a change in status has sometimes led to over- or under-payments. Several London boroughs reported that asylum-seeking households in temporary accommodation lost their housing benefit entitlement when their claim was rejected and that it was often some time before these boroughs were alerted to the problem [BOX E]. Sometimes this led to irrecoverable rent arrears. Officers also reported immense difficulty in contacting the IND by telephone to confirm people's status. Lack of guidance from other government departments is equally problematic; several health authorities and education departments expressed concern over the lack of good practice guidance from the Department of Health (DoH) and the Department for Education and Employment (DfEE). The British Medical Association (BMA) has stressed that there is an urgent need for guidelines for health authorities and doctors treating asylum seekers and refugees (Ref. 15).

39. The introduction of new arrangements presents an opportunity to tackle these problems. The recently established interdepartmental policy forum – bringing together the relevant government departments – is a positive step. It is a means of establishing protocols for information-sharing and effective notification procedures between government departments and, in turn, from government departments to local agencies. A top priority is to ensure timely notification by IND to NASS and claimants (and, where appropriate, the Benefits Agency) of changes in claimants' status. This will, in turn, generate information from NASS to local agencies so that removal or move-on from NASS accommodation can be managed effectively. The forum should also consider what guidance could be provided on how the needs of asylum seekers and refugees can be met locally.

BOX E

Impact of failure to share information

A Croatian doctor who arrived in London from Zagreb in 1993 claimed housing benefit and income support for herself and her daughter. IND reached a negative decision on her application in December 1997 but failed to inform her, so she continued to claim housing benefit until March 1998. She accumulated an overpayment of over £4,000, which the council's housing benefit section sought to recover; negotiations are in hand to repay the sum owed in weekly instalments. On appeal, she was granted exceptional leave to remain, making her eligible for housing benefit again.

Source: Audit Commission fieldwork

Developing a strategic approach

40. Consortia should prepare a strategy to guide their overall direction in the medium and longer term, incorporating aims and priorities for local services. Few councils yet have a profile of asylum seeker and refugee communities in their area, nor an inter-agency strategy that is designed to meet their needs comprehensively [**EXHIBIT 5**]. Although a number of local authorities are beginning to prepare strategies, the pressure of day-to-day operational issues has constrained long-term, multi-agency planning. So far, only a limited range of external stakeholders has been involved in strategic development [**EXHIBIT 6, overleaf**]. The picture is no better in health authorities. None of the health authorities visited had a strategy for refugees and asylum seekers; instead, planning for service provision tends to be addressed within ethnic health and homelessness strategies. A better response is evident in areas with a high density of refugee population and those English authorities with Health Action Zone initiatives. Those dispersed more widely often receive little or no commissioning attention. Regional consortia are well placed to bridge these gaps and develop a strategic response. Through joint working, they should aim to identify the needs of new arrivals, as well as those of their existing refugee and asylum seeker communities, and determine what each agency can do to meet them within their resources.

EXHIBIT 5

Planning to meet asylum seekers' and refugees' needs

Few councils yet have a profile of asylum seeker and refugee communities in their area or a strategy to meet their needs.

Local authorities were asked: *Has your authority carried out a needs assessment of asylum seekers/refugees in its area?* and *Does your authority have a council-wide strategy for asylum seekers and refugees?*

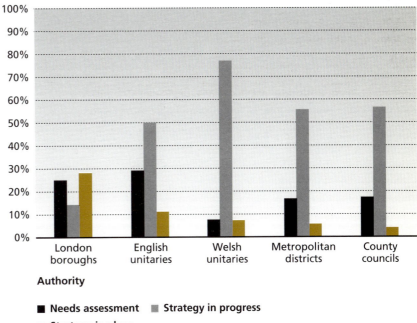

Percentage of authorities

Authority

■ **Needs assessment**   ■ **Strategy in progress**
■ **Strategy in place**

Note: Percentages are based on 97 authorities who responded to the question on needs assessment. All (101) respondents answered the strategy question.

Source: Audit Commission survey

EXHIBIT 6

External stakeholders' involvement in strategy development.

So far only a limited range of external stakeholders have been involved in strategic development.

Local authorities were asked: *Which external stakeholders were involved in developing a council-wide strategy for asylum seekers and refugees?*

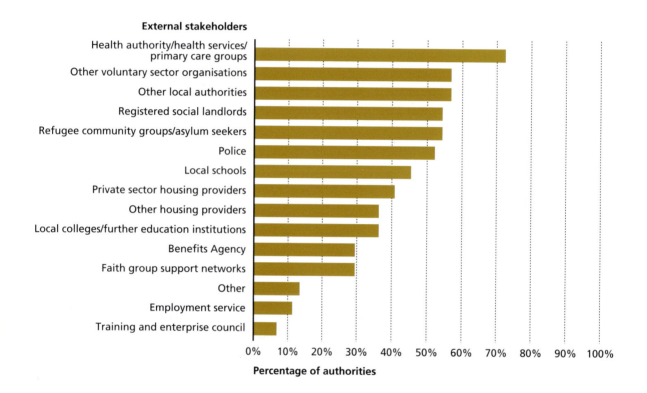

Note: Percentages are based on responses from 44 authorities.

Source: Audit Commission survey

Needs analysis

41. Asylum seekers are a heterogeneous group with different social experiences – their needs will vary according to age, gender, nationality and ethnic background. To be effective, consortia strategies should be informed by data on the composition and profile of local asylum seekers and refugees. They should also take into account the current circumstances in any new arrivals' country of origin, and the type of problems that they are likely to face in the UK [CASE STUDY 1]. There could be important differences between groups from the same country, as they may have been on opposing sides of a conflict before their arrival in the UK. And finally, the priorities of new arrivals and more established refugee communities could diverge. Security, food and shelter are typically the most pressing concerns of new asylum seekers, while employment and training opportunities are important for more settled groups.

CASE STUDY 1

Identifying the needs of refugees and asylum seekers: Cardiff County Council

In partnership with the Welsh Refugee Council, Cardiff County Council identified what problems typically face refugees and asylum seekers and showed how services could respond effectively to:

- the stress of obtaining asylum or refugee status;
- language and cultural barriers;
- unfamiliarity with UK systems, including how local government works;
- physical health problems, such as malnutrition or the effects of torture;
- mental distress, depression or trauma;
- lack of family or community support and isolation;
- limited access to jobs and training;
- homelessness and unsuitable housing;
- poverty in the country of arrival;
- loss of personal wealth in the country of origin; and
- racial harassment, violence and discrimination.

Source: Audit Commission fieldwork

42. Consortia cannot assess local needs with any degree of confidence if they are uncertain about the profile of new arrivals and lack information about the demographic and social profile of existing asylum seekers and refugees at both local and national levels. Several sources of national and local information can provide a partial picture (see Appendix 4). Surveys, focus groups, peer research or conferences to seek the views of new arrivals and those asylum seekers, refugees and their community groups already living within the area, are effective techniques deployed by a number of authorities to build up a more comprehensive picture [**CASE STUDY 2**].

CASE STUDY 2

Identifying needs through peer group surveys: Royal Borough of Kensington and Chelsea

With finance from the National Lottery Charities Board and the Save the Children Fund, the Royal Borough of Kensington and Chelsea undertook a peer research project with young refugees and asylum seekers in the area. A group of seven young people from the Horn of Africa Youth Scheme carried out semi-structured interviews with 34 of their peers in secondary education, as well as local education professionals, to identify the support needs of asylum-seeking children in schools.

Among the group's findings were:

- almost two-thirds of interviewees had started school mid-year, and one-third had attended more than one school in Britain – sometimes because they had moved from place to place;
- over three-quarters had been shown around the school but most felt unable to ask any questions because of poor English or nervousness;
- only one-quarter had received any information about the British education system when they arrived in the country and nearly all felt it would have been useful to receive information, including advice on choosing different subjects and where to get support in learning English;
- nearly all got English language support at school and two-thirds were satisfied with it; those dissatisfied felt that the support was insufficient or inappropriate;
- one-third wanted more help with homework, including homework clubs; and
- one-half were aware of bullying in their schools and one in seven had themselves been bullied.

The peer review approach gave the council an insight into the issues from the children's perspective, and overcame problems of cultural differences between researchers and those being interviewed. The language skills of the researchers also allowed some interviews to be conducted in the children's native tongue.

Source: Audit Commission fieldwork

...consortia should enhance local information systems in order to strengthen needs assessment and strategy development.

43. In the longer term, consortia should enhance local information systems in order to strengthen needs assessment and strategy development. Better information about the use of local services by asylum seekers would provide a firmer basis for forecasting demand and identifying access problems. While there are obvious sensitivities about collecting information on the use of services based on immigration status, such services cannot be planned, evaluated or costed without hard information about current usage. Nor is it possible to identify whether asylum seekers face emerging problems that agencies will need to prioritise, such as a higher than average proportion of special educational needs statements or school exclusions among asylum-seeking children. Few of the authorities visited could provide information of this type. At a national level, new computerised information systems in NASS and the IND could offer useful information for local decision making, providing that information is passed to regional consortia.

Review of existing provision

44. Alongside needs analysis, a review of existing local services will give consortia a clear picture of the capacity of local agencies to meet the new demands arising from dispersal and, equally importantly, to identify any gaps in service provision. It should also provide an opportunity to review the outcomes and impact of previous initiatives, such as those that were put in place during the Kosovan Humanitarian Evacuation Programme, identifying the lessons learned. It may be appropriate to repeat some of these initiatives for new arrivals.

Strategic choices and priorities

45. On the basis of the information assembled, consortia will be able to identify the actions required of each consortium partner. With limited resources, tough choices may arise about the type of initiatives to pursue – it will not be possible to develop a wide range of support services from day one. Instead, consortia will have to plan over a longer timescale – of, say, five years – and focus initially on immediate requirements. In doing this, they will need to take into account the costs of different options relative to their expected benefits, as well as their long-term sustainability, and establish targets that allow performance to be monitored.

Involving elected members

46. Political support is critical to the successful implementation of local dispersal arrangements. The degree of member support will undoubtedly vary, both across and within authorities, but participation in the consortia can help members to articulate the concerns of their authority and local residents and influence policy choices. As consortia representatives, members can also:

- provide a link between the regional consortium and their council, so that key issues and decisions are widely understood;

- help to assess the impact of consortium policy on their own residents and services; and

- act as recognised spokespersons in their own authority to ensure that key messages across the region are consistent.

47. Member involvement should not be limited to representation on the consortium. They can advise on the suitability of individual locations for asylum seekers, welcome new arrivals (for example, in ward newsletters) and host local community events. In the longer term, they may also help to resolve tensions that can arise between existing residents and asylum-seeking communities. In one authority, a ward member responded to complaints that asylum seekers were leaving rubbish in their gardens by hiring a community skip for both asylum seekers and residents to use over a weekend. Seminars and briefings are useful vehicles for involving a wider range of members and building understanding across all political parties. In one authority visited, this approach led to a cross-party alliance on asylum seekers and refugees that helped to convey consistent political messages across the authority.

48. Equity between local residents and asylum-seeking and refugee communities, or between different communities of asylum seekers and refugees, is an important consideration for elected members. Research for this study found significant variations in access to, and quality of, service provision among different groups [BOX F]. Unsurprisingly, this has generated community tensions and reinforced hostility towards new arrivals. There may well be a need for differential services, but the reasons for this should be explained by members and officers.

BOX F

Inequities in service provision

- Some schools refuse to provide school places for asylum seekers, even though it is generally a legal requirement if they have places available.

- In one authority visited, asylum seekers housed under social services legislation were provided with funds for furniture and household equipment, whereas those housed under homelessness legislation were not.

- One authority routinely provided taxis to transport asylum seekers to newly allocated accommodation – other homeless families had to rely on public transport.

- One authority had a rent deposit scheme to help asylum seekers to secure private rented accommodation; no similar scheme existed for other homeless people.

Source: Audit Commission fieldwork

Proactive management of community relations

49. The Kosovan Humanitarian Evacuation Programme showed that positive, well-organised media briefings help to generate public support, particularly when reinforced by positive messages at a national level. On the other hand, negative press coverage can inflame local public opinion and create a climate in which fair treatment is hard to achieve. At present, press coverage of asylum seekers is overwhelmingly negative. The Commission analysed 161 local press articles collated by the Refugee Council in October/November 1999: only 6 per cent cited the positive contribution made by asylum seekers and refugees; 28 per cent focused on the housing and/or employment difficulties attributed to this group; and 15 per cent concerned crimes and offences committed by asylum seekers.[1] Devising a local press and publicity strategy prior to receiving asylum seekers can help to create more positive coverage, not least by ensuring that both local communities and the media have accurate and balanced information [**CASE STUDY 3**].

---

1   The analysis considered both the tone and the content of the articles. Tone was classified as negative, positive or neutral and took into account the language used – for example, negative language included terms such as flood, burden, bogus and dumping/shipping. The content was categorised as follows: contributions made by refugees/asylum seekers; crime/housing/employment/education problems associated with refugees/asylum seekers; community or racial tension/violence; and projects to support asylum seekers.

CASE STUDY 3

A joint media and public relations strategy: Yorkshire and Humberside Consortium

The Yorkshire and Humberside consortium has developed a joint media and public relations strategy to address local media interest in asylum seekers dispersed to the region. Building upon links developed during the Kosovan programme, the strategy includes:

- **clear aims** – the consortium wants to promote a positive and accurate view of dispersal;

- **operational arrangements** – one authority will serve as the contact point for regional issues; each local authority has a link person to network press coverage of local stories;

- **a proactive approach** – to generate positive press coverage of dispersal, including arranging interviews with selected asylum seekers on behalf of the media;

- **key messages** – developing guidance to promote consistent messages and to deal with difficult questions; and

- **briefings** – ensuring that all local agencies and their workers know how to route proactive stories and reactive enquiries to a single contact point.

Work undertaken so far has already generated positive media coverage in the region and asylum seekers and refugees have spoken about their experiences to journalists; this has helped to promote positive messages about new arrivals.

Source: Audit Commission fieldwork

50. The success of a local public relations campaign will be highly dependent upon both the extent to which all agencies and authorities are signed up to the approach adopted, and the active involvement of their senior officers. Evidence from the Commission's fieldwork also highlighted the value of:

- getting the local press involved early, and stressing the need for coverage to be handled sensitively and responsibly;

- linking partners' press offices so that consistent messages can be promoted;

- briefing the media before sensitive decisions, such as the location of new arrivals, are made public through committee papers;

- avoiding the use of negative or emotive language – terms such as 'flood' or 'burden' can quickly reinforce public hostility; and

- using the media to promote positive success stories about local asylum seekers and to dispel local myths. In one authority, ill-informed rumours were rife about the additional benefits available to asylum seekers and so the council published details in the local newspaper of the actual sums that they received.

Consortia or councils should consider the implications of asylum seekers' involvement in a press and public relations strategy. Their participation often helps to convey the human issues surrounding asylum, but some asylum seekers who make public statements may face hostility from local groups, or may cause problems for family members still in their country of origin.

51. A positive press and public relations strategy can be supplemented by other initiatives designed to promote good community relations and increase understanding between asylum seekers and the local population. Two authorities visited had jointly appointed a community development officer, partly to address emerging problems between local residents and asylum seekers [CASE STUDY 4]. In another area, tensions between local residents and asylum seekers were reduced when councillors hosted two public meetings that allowed local people to air their concerns, but at the same time gave asylum seekers a chance to put forward their case. Consortia should also consider notifying existing residents' and tenants' organisations of plans to move asylum seekers into their area, although not necessarily identifying the specific properties. Almost 80 per cent of authorities do not routinely do this, although it can be a useful way of increasing understanding and support among local people before asylum seekers move into their area.

CASE STUDY 4

Partnership working to promote community relations: Kent County Council and Dover District Council

Kent County Council and Dover District Council established a jointly funded community liaison officer post in 1998. The officer is a link between asylum seekers, local residents and service providers in the area, promoting joint working between the two tiers of local government and addressing concerns raised by local residents. Working in partnership with other statutory and voluntary agencies, this officer has facilitated a number of new initiatives, including:

- discussions and seminars to increase awareness of asylum seeker issues among professional groups and local agencies;

- a Holiday Friendship scheme, bringing local school children together with asylum-seeking children through project work and outings;

- an afternoon drop-in centre run in partnership with the local church;

- weekly English language classes run by the local church;

- an information booklet for asylum seekers, available in appropriate languages;

- work with Dover Residents Against Racism to develop a recreation and social centre for young male asylum seekers; and

- English and IT classes in a local hotel used by asylum seekers, run in partnership with South Kent College and Kent County Council adult education department.

Source: Audit Commission fieldwork

52. Sensitive policing approaches can also help to ease community tensions, and local authorities and police forces should, where relevant, encompass the new arrangements in their crime and disorder reduction strategies. Kent County Constabulary analysed a range of local incidents involving asylum seekers to identify the key issues that were relevant to policing. New approaches were developed to tackle problems of crime and disorder and to respond positively to the presence of asylum seekers; these included building an asylum seekers' brief into the role of existing police officers [CASE STUDY 5]. One month after the implementation of the new approach, reported racial incidents dropped by over 20 per cent. The Association of Chief Police Officers is currently preparing a good practice guide for the policing of asylum seekers and refugee communities, drawing upon the experience of Kent and other forces.

CASE STUDY 5

Policing asylum seekers: Kent County Constabulary

In 1999, Kent County Constabulary spent £1.95 million policing those areas with significant numbers of asylum seekers. Following a number of violent incidents between asylum seekers and local residents in Dover and Gravesend, Kent analysed the factors underlying local tensions. Recurrent problems included:

- fear of authority by asylum seekers, leading to unreported racial attacks and an unwillingness to report crime;
- lack of integration of asylum seekers into the local community and consequent cultural conflict;
- emotive and sensational media reporting;

- poor communication between statutory agencies, resident communities and asylum seekers; and
- inadequate information both about racist offenders and the profile of asylum seekers living in the area.

In response, the role of Kent's Race and Community Relations Officer was reviewed, and the post now has a more specific focus on asylum seekers. This has included profiling asylum-seeking communities in the South East Kent police area, and developing new community links. Initiatives have included:

- running multi-agency fora at a strategic and operational level;
- visiting hotels and hostels to build trust;

- holding a weekly police surgery for asylum seekers;
- translating the Public Order Act (Section 5) warning card, to prevent unnecessary arrests; and
- training local officers on the rights, customs and cultures of asylum-seeking communities.

Officers within other police teams have also been given more explicit roles. For example, a dedicated investigator now investigates all racial crimes and feeds information back to the Intelligence Unit. A nominated field intelligence officer identifies offenders and offending within the asylum communities, and profiles possible threats to asylum seekers from the local community.

Source: Audit Commission, based on information from Kent County Constabulary

Overcoming barriers to service delivery

53. Asylum seekers face considerable barriers in accessing services, often because they do not understand how local services work. As the Refugee Council notes, *We tend to assume that UK services are easy to understand. But for an asylum seeker the system may appear very complicated or illogical, and it is often unclear who is responsible for what* (Ref. 16). Other common problems include language barriers, a lack of information about what services are available, low staff awareness and a lack of cash. Consortia can help to tackle these problems by providing better information to asylum seekers, training staff, and developing interpreting services. It will also be important to address barriers to services that may arise through the new voucher scheme.

Information

54. On arrival in an area, asylum seekers need basic information in their own languages about their rights and entitlements to services, the facilities available in their accommodation, and local details such as the nearest hospital or post office. NASS will advise asylum seekers which post office will issue their vouchers, which local retailers will accept them, and will provide information about the local one-stop shop advice service. Information about services that they can access free of charge is also helpful; one asylum seeker interviewed by the Commission said it would have been useful to know that many art galleries, museums and libraries do not charge for entry. Others suggested that maps of local areas and services, and details of local community groups would have been helpful.

55. To minimise costs, more use could be made of information leaflets already produced by the Refugee Council. Other information could also be produced nationally. Information about asylum seekers' entitlement to health services and a simple explanation of how the UK health system operates, for example, could be produced jointly by the DoH and NASS and issued to all new arrivals. This could help to ensure that consistent, high-quality information is available in a greater number of languages; a format could also be developed to include local information.

56. Some asylum seekers are unwilling to assert their rights, particularly in requesting additional services or making complaints. They may feel that they should be grateful for any service provided, regardless of its quality, or fear that a complaint will adversely affect their asylum claim. To address this, agencies should aim to provide new arrivals with information about the standards of service that they can expect and copies of complaints procedures in their own languages.

Staff training

57. Few councils visited during the Commission's fieldwork had trained staff to raise their awareness of the needs of asylum seekers and refugees, or their rights and entitlements to services. Some managers assumed that staff were qualified to work with asylum seekers simply because they were part of the same ethnic group, or had once worked in the country of origin of more recent arrivals. Authorities should draw upon a wide range of published information that offers guidance to health practitioners, schools and training and employment advisers, which is summarised in a recent guide produced by the Refugee Council (Ref 16). Training can be undertaken in partnership with local refugee community organisations or national refugee groups. Individual agencies should also consider whether their existing equal opportunities and racial harassment policies need revision to reflect their responsibilities towards asylum seekers and refugees.

Interpretation and translation

58. Helping asylum seekers to overcome language barriers and gain access to services requires the use of interpreters and the provision of written material in various languages. Three types of interpretation service are commonly used, each with strengths and weaknesses [BOX G]. There is no rule about when to use a particular method, and judgement has to be applied to fit the situation. For example, a commercial 24-hour telephone interpreting service may be the best means to establish factual information quickly. When sensitive issues have to be explored in some depth, trained interpreters will allow for a more personal approach, offer more precise linguistic skills and prove more cost effective. Generally speaking, children should not be used as interpreters; while they may pick up English more quickly than their parents, it is inappropriate to use them as intermediaries when discussing topics that would not ordinarily be discussed with a child.

59. Since access to interpreters is likely to be limited in some of the dispersal areas, consortia will need to develop interpretation services, and review whether existing staff have language skills that can be used. In one mental health trust the languages spoken by staff have been listed in the internal telephone directory. Training staff to work with interpreters is also important, building upon good practice issued by the Refugee Council [BOX H, overleaf]. Training asylum seekers as interpreters could also help to bridge gaps in provision and ensure a rapid response to sudden influxes of arrivals with new language needs. The London Borough of Lewisham is running a project to provide asylum seekers with an accredited qualification in community translation that offers a route to the Institute of Linguists qualification. The project is a joint initiative with Lewisham Refugee Network, which helps to recruit students, and Lewisham College, and is part funded by the European Social Fund. As restrictions on volunteering may prevent some asylum seekers without permission to work from using the skills that they develop through such schemes, the Government should consider whether current restrictions on all or specific types of voluntary activity for asylum seekers should be lifted.

BOX G

The advantages and disadvantages of different types of interpretation facilities

METHOD	ADVANTAGES	DISADVANTAGES
24–hour telephone interpreting service	• Services can usually be accessed at short notice • Covers a wide range of languages (around 40) • Confidentiality maintained	• Interpreters may not be familiar with services for asylum seekers and may vary in quality • Inability to assess non-verbal communication or third party interference • High cost (£3 per minute)
Trained interpreters	• Familiarity with service terminology and background • Enables more personal, lengthy exchanges • Face-to-face contacts can help to build trust with the client • Quality of provision can be monitored	• Service may be difficult to arrange at short notice • May be difficult to access the full range of languages required • Supply shortages may lead to increased costs
Refugee or asylum-seeker community interpreters	• Low cost • Familiarity may offer reassurance and support to the client • Offers opportunity for local asylum seekers to develop their skills and confidence	• Confidentiality may not be assured • Clients may not wish to divulge information in the presence of family/community members • May not be trained interpreters

Source: Audit Commission

BOX H

Working with interpreters: Refugee Council guidance

- Use interpreters even if the client speaks some English – misunderstandings are common.

- Do not rely on other family members or children to act as interpreters – it may not be appropriate to discuss certain subjects in front of relatives.

- Provide staff training on how to work with interpreters.

- Check that the interpreter and the client speak the same language or dialect.

- Allow time for a pre-interview discussion with the interpreter to explain the content of the interview and how you will work together.

- Ask the interpreter to explain about the policy of confidentiality.

- Actively listen to both the interpreter and the client.

- Use simple language.

- Check that the client is happy with the interpreters provided.

- Allow extra time for the appointment/interview – it will take longer than those without an interpreter.

- At the end, make sure that the client has understood everything, ask whether s/he has any questions.

- Have a post-interview discussion with the interpreter.

Source: Refugee Council (Ref. 16)

60. The need to provide interpretation and translate information will represent a new demand on the budgets of many authorities. The Commission's survey found that 37 per cent of councils do not have translation and interpreting services and 55 per cent do not produce written material in languages other than English. Costs could be minimised by developing joint interpretation and translation facilities or common pricing structures between local agencies. In anticipation of increased demand for local interpreters, for example, one consortium has agreed a common pricing structure across all agencies in its region. These sorts of arrangements may, however, need to be revised over time as language needs may change. Under the voluntary dispersal arrangements, many authorities outside London struggled to meet the language needs of mixed groups. One authority commented upon the communication difficulties presented by its first group of new arrivals, who came from 12 different countries. If a shortage of accommodation means that dispersal cannot be organised around language 'clusters', these problems will persist.

Life without cash

61. New arrivals will have access to very little cash and will be largely dependent upon vouchers. Although these will be valid in a range of retail outlets, they will not, unlike other social security benefits, offer an automatic passport to other local services. For example, entitlement to benefits can also mean free entry or reduced charges to local sports centres. Some authorities are developing schemes to overcome these problems. Liverpool City Council, for example, runs a reception centre for new arrivals and has developed a pass scheme to allow asylum seekers who are residents of the centre to use a local sports centre. A token sum of 20 pence is paid for each group pass, which is available from staff at the reception centre. The council hopes to extend the initiative to those who have moved out to alternative accommodation.

Rights and entitlements – national action

62. Although most barriers to services can be overcome locally, action is needed at a national level to clarify the rights and entitlements of asylum seekers. For example, local difficulties often arise from the documentation issued to new arrivals either at the port of entry or at IND offices. In a number of cases, new arrivals have been issued with compliment slips rather than standard acknowledgement letters (SALs), making frontline staff understandably cautious about their entitlements. The consistent use of standard documentation, ideally including a comprehensive 'rights statement', would resolve such difficulties. The National Association of Citizens Advice Bureaux (NACAB) recommends that, when the Home Office sends notification of a new, extended or otherwise varied immigration status to an asylum applicant, a summary of the principal rights associated with that status should be attached (Ref. 17). These would not be statements related to named individuals, but rather a summary of rights and entitlements for each immigration status. NACAB suggests that the Home Office could issue these to people at the port of arrival and send them to someone when they are notified in writing of their immigration status.

Promoting refugee community development and involvement

63. Involving local refugees and asylum seekers and refugee community organisations (RCOs) can help local agencies to deliver services more effectively and to avoid costly mistakes. It can also help to build confidence and self-esteem among asylum seekers and improve their understanding of the services that are available. Despite these benefits, consultation with refugees and asylum seekers is currently limited. The Audit Commission's survey found that, even in London, only about one-half of authorities had consulted refugee communities in order to inform service planning in the past year. Other more formal mechanisms for meeting this client group are also limited; only 35 of the authorities surveyed have a formal refugee working party that meets on a regular basis. Where such groups do exist, it does not necessarily follow that they provide a vehicle for genuine consultation and participation in decision making. One refugee agency felt that the council working party was a conduit for information rather than an opportunity to influence decision making.

64. By bringing together a range of agencies, regional consortia have an opportunity to promote greater refugee-community involvement and to pioneer new approaches that fully reflect the complexities of consulting asylum seekers and refugees [BOX I]. In doing so, it will be important to

---

BOX I

Consulting refugees and asylum seekers

CONSULTATION	ISSUES TO CONSIDER	
Language barriers	• Translation of written material and/or interpreters will be required to support non-English speakers.	✔
Cultural issues	• Religious holidays, such as Ramadan, should be avoided and food and drink provision should be culturally sensitive at meetings.	✔
Gender balance	• In cultures where men usually act as spokespersons, women's views may need to be sought separately.	✔
Representation	• Different nationalities, or groups within the same nationality, may need to be consulted separately. • The concerns of asylum seekers and those with more settled status may differ.	✔
Consultation methods	• In some cultures, written forms of consultation may not be effective; Somalis, for example, have an oral tradition so face-to-face discussion may be more appropriate.	✔
Confidentiality	• Some individuals may distrust authority or be concerned that expressing negative views will affect their asylum claim – assurances of confidentiality will need to be given to encourage them to speak freely.	✔
Childcare and transport	• Providing an on-site crèche at meetings or transport to venues could increase participation.	✔

Source: Audit Commission

build trust with participants, many of whom may distrust authority. Often, local authorities negotiate access through an established community leader or seek the views of RCOs on a delegate basis. This is not an adequate substitute for consulting individuals, particularly as new arrivals may not have a refugee community organisation to represent them. The effectiveness of different initiatives should also be carefully evaluated – there is little point repeating a consultation if the costs outweigh the benefits.[1]

65. RCOs can relieve pressure on local agencies by filling gaps in service delivery, as well as providing a channel of communication and support by:

- helping new arrivals with vital matters relating to integration;

- providing psychological and material support;

- helping maintain their own community's cultural identity;

- promoting a positive image among nationals of their host country through their representations; and

- providing an opportunity for meaningful activity to enhance the self-image of refugees (Ref. 18).

66. Currently, RCOs are concentrated largely in London; a recent directory located 88 per cent of the existing 259 RCOs in London (Ref. 19). As a consequence, London-based RCOs are facing increased demands on their time and resources from service providers in other parts of the country, often to meet a need for urgent interpretation services for new arrivals dispersed under voluntary arrangements. This is not sustainable in the long term – these organisations are often reliant on volunteers and face their own funding constraints.

67. Consortia should, therefore, try to secure funding to support the development of RCOs outside London. Individual agencies should also review their grant criteria to ensure that funds can be accessed by emerging refugee groups, many of which will inevitably struggle to pay for premises and day-to-day running costs. So far, local authorities have provided little financial support – of the 101 authorities that responded to the Audit Commission's survey, only 22 funded RCOs, and over one-half of those were in London. The number of groups funded ranged from 1 to 13, and the total funding provided varied from £500 to £399,500. Some financial support may also be available to RCOs from national sources, such as the National Lottery Charities Board and Home Office Race Equality Unit grant programme. Some £2.5 million will be available from the latter in 2000/01, and a further £5 million in 2001/02; the Home Office and consortia should make information on these funds available to local groups.

---

1   Further guidance on consultation methods, including when and how to use them, can be found in the Audit Commission's recent publication, *Listen Up*.

Conclusion

68. To date, the needs of asylum seekers and refugees have not been addressed in a systematic way. Operational pressures, combined with scant information and inadequate joint working, have too often impeded a strategic approach. Despite some examples of innovative good practice, many barriers to services and inequities in service provision persist. The new regional consortia have an opportunity to improve the situation. As multi-agency partnerships, they are well placed to promote a more strategic approach across their region and address gaps in services and information [EXHIBIT 7]. In doing so, they need to reflect the political sensitivities surrounding dispersal by building political and community support in their areas. To support the consortia, the Government should improve information flows between relevant departments and local agencies, and consider how national messages on asylum and immigration policy influence the responses of local communities when new arrivals are sent to their area.

EXHIBIT 7

The roles of regional consortia

Regional consortia will need to develop strategies drawing together resources, knowledge and expertise in local agencies to provide a comprehensive support package for new arrivals.

Source: Audit Commission

3

Providing Support Services at the Local Level

The quantity, range and quality of services for asylum seekers and refugees varies across England and Wales. Shortfalls in key services – such as legal advice and English language support – tend to be more acute in areas with little experience of this client group. Local agencies need to consider carefully how they can develop services to meet the needs of new arrivals. Without effective support services, asylum seekers could easily become locked in a cycle of exclusion and dependency in their new community.

69. Asylum seekers placed in a local area will require a diverse range of services to support them from arrival to settlement [**EXHIBIT 8**]. While not all new arrivals will have higher levels of need than the indigenous population, some services will probably need to be adapted if they are to be accessible and relevant to them. But services such as legal advice and interpretation will be in higher demand and providers should consider how local provision can be developed to meet this need. Some groups – such as the elderly, disabled people and people with HIV/AIDS – will also have special needs. This chapter looks at the steps that providers should take to meet the needs of asylum seekers and refugees; it highlights problems that are often experienced by this group, and offers examples of good practice in providing:

- housing and support;
- legal services;
- health services;
- social services support for unaccompanied minors;
- education for school-age children;
- English language support; and
- employment and training.

EXHIBIT 8

Key services from arrival to settlement

Asylum seekers who are placed in a local area will need access to a wide range of services to support them from arrival to settlement.

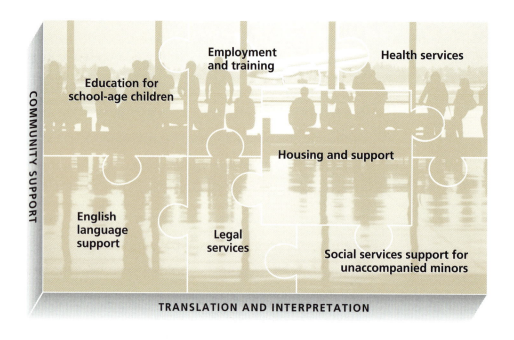

Source: Audit Commission

Housing and support

70. The new Act imposes a general duty upon both local authorities and registered social landlords (RSLs) in England and Wales to assist the Secretary of State in providing accommodation for asylum seekers where 'reasonable in the circumstances' (Ref. 20). The scale of housing provision required by NASS in the first year of dispersal is considerable – in 2000/01, it has been estimated that 37,120 units of accommodation will be needed (Ref. 22). NASS will provide emergency accommodation for those asylum seekers who have no other means of support on arrival; those whom they agree to support will then be dispersed to accommodation in one of the consortia areas. NASS expects to contract with consortia to provide 40 per cent of the provision required, whether from local authorities, RSLs or private sector landlords [BOX J]. NASS intends to contract directly with social housing providers or private landlords to provide the remaining 60 per cent of units, but in practice this 40:60 ratio may vary.

BOX J

Provision of accommodation through consortia: NASS terms and conditions

In February 2000, the Local Government Association informed regional consortia lead officers and housing directors that NASS had indicated that it would secure council accommodation on the following terms:

- accommodation will be contracted to NASS for a period of three to five years;
- occupancy is guaranteed from the date the contract comes into effect;
- authorities can charge for start-up refurbishment and equipment costs, and for the cost of replacement furniture and equipment;
- utilities costs should be charged on the basis of £20 per household per week;
- the charge to NASS should include provision for the recovery of council rent and council tax;
- in some instances, single adults will be expected to share accommodation;
- a ratio of three single adults to one family should be assumed.

For illustrative purposes, it was suggested that consortia could allow a charge of up to £20 per week per property to cover their overheads and £20 per week per case to cover 'other services' that are likely to be required. Actual sums paid would be subject to negotiation with NASS.

Source: Letter from LGA to regional consortia lead officers (Ref. 21) *and correspondence from NASS* (Ref. 22)

71. The decision to phase in the new support arrangements from April 2000 was triggered by the shortfall in the units of accommodation secured by NASS; by the end of January 2000, less than 10 per cent of the number required had been identified. A number of reasons have been put forward to explain this shortfall:

- political concerns that the full cost of support for asylum seekers would not be met by the Government, potentially leading to increases in council tax;

- the complexity of the contracting process, coupled with delays in issuing paperwork to the consortia, which may have delayed the preparation of bids;

- the performance measures or terms and conditions included in contracts which may have been unacceptable to some potential providers (Ref. 23);

- available accommodation in consortia areas may not have met the broad criteria for dispersal; and

- the lack of information about bids being put forward by other housing providers independently of the consortia, making it impossible for consortia to forecast the overall level of demand on other support services, and to finalise their own plans.

72. Whatever the precise reasons for the shortfall, the success of the new policy will be dependent upon an adequate supply of housing. To play its part, each consortium needs to work with potential providers within the partnership and:

- identify suitable locations for asylum seekers within its region;

- determine what type of housing and support to provide;

- consider how permanent accommodation can be provided for asylum seekers whose applications are approved;

- decide the best way to manage those who lose their entitlement to housing following a negative decision; and

- assess the financial viability of the housing role.

Each of these issues is examined in detail below.

Identifying suitable locations to house asylum seekers

73. Ideally, a broad range of criteria should be taken into account when identifying suitable locations for asylum seekers [BOX K], but realistically few areas will meet all (or even the majority of) these criteria in the short term. Different problems could emerge in different locations. While multi-cultural areas offer better community networks and minimise racial tension, accommodation may be concentrated on run-down housing estates with few employment opportunities and over-stretched public services. Placement in such areas would risk compounding the exclusion of asylum seekers and may heighten deprivation in the host community. And yet placing asylum seekers in areas that are not multi-racial can also create problems. One fieldwork authority housed 30 Somalian families on an outlying, predominantly white, estate. Within a few years, all but three families had left because of harassment from other residents and isolation from their own community groups, which were concentrated in the town centre. Locations that are likely to pose intractable problems for asylum seekers and need to be avoided completely should be identified by consortia.

BOX K

Factors to consider when assessing whether areas are suitable for asylum seekers

CONSIDER	ASK	
Ethnic composition	• Does the area have a multi-cultural population? • Does the area already include people of the same nationality as the asylum seekers?	✔
Community relations	• Is there likely to be conflict between different groups of asylum seekers from the same country? • Does the area have a history of racial tension? • Is the placement of asylum seekers and refugees likely to lead to tension?	✘
Community networks	• Are there established refugee community groups in the area? • Is there support available to develop new community networks?	✔
School places	• Are there school places available for asylum-seeking children? • Is language support available in these schools?	✔
Translation and interpretation services	• Are there adequate translation and interpretation facilities in the local area?	✔
Legal support	• Is the area well served by immigration lawyers?	✔
Employment opportunities	• Is the area likely to offer asylum seekers and refugees employment opportunities in the longer term?	✔
Places of worship	• Are there places of worship to meet the religious needs of asylum seekers?	✔
Other services	• Will asylum seekers be within walking distance of other services, such as local colleges, health services and outlets accepting vouchers? • Is the area well-served by public transport? • Do local services, such as GPs, have the capacity to meet the needs of both asylum seekers and the indigenous community?	✔

Source: Audit Commission

...housing support programmes will need to anticipate the type of problems that asylum seekers may face...

74. Since few areas will fulfil all of these criteria, housing support programmes will need to anticipate the type of problems that asylum seekers may face and identify ways of mitigating them. The Housing Corporation has developed a useful model (Housing Plus) to promote community sustainability that could be adapted to meet the needs of asylum seekers who are placed on 'difficult-to-let' estates (Ref. 24). It involves devising a community action plan that seeks to match the social and demographic profile of tenants to community facilities, and to identify initiatives to combat social exclusion and poverty. Particularly when developed in consultation with tenants and other partners, such plans can underpin initiatives that are designed to improve asylum seekers' (and other residents') quality of life, including childcare projects, mediation services to resolve conflict between residents, leisure facilities and community safety schemes. Funding from the Single Regeneration Budget (SRB) or European programmes may be available for new projects.

75. Providers also need to consider the implications that ring fencing stock for asylum seekers may have for applicants on their housing waiting list and homeless people in the longer term. For example, a council with high demand for family-sized accommodation will need to assess carefully whether the authority could meet a long-term demand for permanent accommodation from families who get refugee status or ELR. There may be a knock-on effect on the private rented sector – the rising number of asylum seekers in London is one factor generating increases in private sector rent levels. Any additional demands on housing stock that may arise through redevelopment programmes should also be assessed, particularly if existing tenants will need to be re-housed.

Types of accommodation and support

76. The pressures on housing stock in London have forced councils to house many asylum seekers in what they know is unsuitable accommodation. For example, the Commission's survey found that over one-third of family households were in bed and breakfast accommodation, hostels or hotel annexes[1] **[EXHIBIT 9]**. The new arrangements therefore provide an opportunity to improve the quality of housing for this client group.

77. NASS has indicated that the type of accommodation to be provided for asylum seekers may include:

• supported accommodation for groups with special needs, including disabled people and vulnerable families;

• hostels with full board or self-catering facilities; and

• self-contained flats or houses.

---

1   Hotel annexes usually offer access to cooking facilities.

EXHIBIT 9

Types of housing used to accommodate asylum seekers

Over one-third of family households were placed in bed and breakfast accommodation, hostels or hotel annexes in October 1999.

Local authorities were asked: *What types of housing were used to accommodate asylum seekers supported by your authority under the National Assistance Act 1948 or Children Act 1989, as at 31 October 1999?*

Note: Percentages are based on responses from 72 authorities providing data for single adults; 62 authorities for families, 39 authorities for unaccompanied children aged 15 and under; and 55 authorities for those aged 16/17. The percentages for families are based on households, rather than individuals.

Source: Audit Commission survey

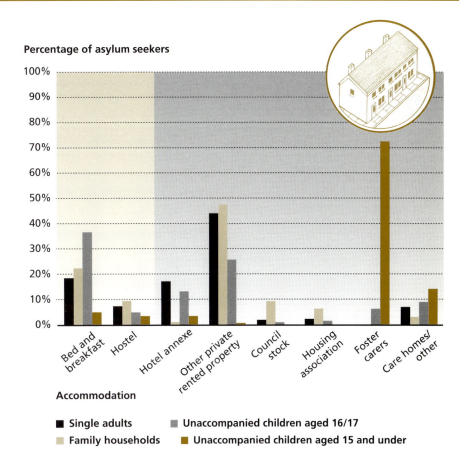

Percentage of asylum seekers

Accommodation

- ■ Single adults
- ■ Family households
- ■ Unaccompanied children aged 16/17
- ■ Unaccompanied children aged 15 and under

78. Although the availability of stock will partially influence what can be offered, NASS should ensure that the needs of different types of asylum-seeking households are taken into account when allocating accommodation. An obvious example is that hostel accommodation that is suitable for single adults may be inappropriate for families, who will fare better in self-contained provision. Where accommodation is self-contained, some grouping of properties will allow for mutual support. In hostel-type accommodation, communal areas and play space for children are important considerations. NASS will specify standards and consortia/local authorities will be consulted about the suitability of accommodation and whether it conforms to local standards. Environmental health officers may need to play a role in checking standards.

79. Housing providers will also need to develop suitable packages of support for asylum seekers, reflecting their higher needs for social support, advocacy and advice. The Housing Corporation has suggested that, on arrival, asylum seekers are likely to require two to three weeks of intensive support, including guidance on basic living skills, services available in the accommodation and local orientation with the area (Ref. 25). Daytime activities and events may help to promote new social networks and counter isolation and boredom among a group with little cash and no immediate right to work. A number of RSLs have already developed relevant programmes, often in conjunction with local colleges, voluntary organisations and businesses [CASE STUDY 6].

Move-on accommodation

80. Asylum seekers who receive a positive decision on their claim become eligible for state benefits and are expected to leave their accommodation within 14 days. Those who receive a negative decision will be able to remain in NASS accommodation while their appeal is being heard. If this appeal is lost, adult asylum seekers will have 14 days to move out of their accommodation, at which time their support package will stop. NASS also expects families who receive a negative decision to leave voluntarily, although some may remain in NASS accommodation until their removal from the UK or until their youngest child reaches 18.

CASE STUDY 6

St Mungo's Housing Association initiative in housing asylum seekers

Working in partnership with the London Borough of Lambeth, St Mungo's Housing Association (SMHA) opened a 61-bedspace hostel for asylum seekers in 1997. As a purpose-built hostel, the property offers many facilities and space for recreation, hobbies and cooking.

Staff members are in daily contact with residents and have developed a number of schemes designed to alleviate some of the financial hardship that they experience. For example, they have recruited a volunteer to fundraise for a hardship fund and to provide residents with resources for essential items such as clothing and shoes. They have also organised day trips and developed special rate admission arrangements with local cinemas and sport centres. Personal computers have been borrowed to help students and those interested in IT.

SMHA also supports an art studio for residents who are interested in painting and to provide therapy for torture victims. A volunteer psychiatrist provides regular in-house surgeries, with a facility to refer people to the Medical Foundation for Victims of Torture.

Source: Housing Corporation (Ref. 25)

81. To avoid homelessness among asylum seekers who receive a positive decision, housing providers need to help them to move quickly to permanent accommodation. For families in 'priority' housing need, this is likely to include the use of alternative local authority or RSL stock. Where families have built an attachment to an area and their children are settled in local schools, there may be a strong argument for allowing them to remain in their existing accommodation, provided that it is suitable for permanent use and replacement stock can be identified for NASS.

82. Single asylum seekers leaving their accommodation after a positive decision will generally be reliant on the private rented sector, but lack of money for a deposit – and some landlords' reluctance to accept housing benefit claimants – may initially make access difficult. Some local authorities have developed rent guarantee and deposit schemes to address this [CASE STUDY 7]. Such schemes are more likely to be successful outside London, in areas where there is less demand for rented accommodation.

CASE STUDY 7

Rent Guarantee Scheme in Lewisham

From September 1996 to March 1998, the Refugee Council, in partnership with the Refugee Arrivals Project and Refugee Housing Association, operated a pilot 'rent-in-advance guarantee scheme' in the London Borough of Lewisham. The aim was to improve refugee access to the private rented sector. Funding was secured via the John Paul Getty Junior Charitable Trust, the Housing Associations Charitable Trust and the Housing Corporation; it included £55,466 in revenue grants and £5,000 in the form of a capital loan for the guarantee fund.

Under the scheme, four weeks' rent in advance was paid to participating landlords and recouped through housing benefit. In lieu of a deposit, a six-month written guarantee was issued to landlords against an agreed inventory of fixtures and fittings. Any subsequent liabilities were then met by the fund, up to agreed limits. Both properties and landlords were vetted prior to participation in the scheme. Landlords and tenants also received practical support and guidance covering issues such as housing benefit services, tenancy agreements, property standards and language and communication needs.

A total of 21 people were housed under the scheme and no claims were made on the guarantee fund. The scheme's evaluation report noted that its overall success had been highly dependent upon good liaison and working relationships with individual housing benefit officers.

Source: Refugee Council (Ref. 26)

...for most housing providers, the 14-day period is too short a time to prioritise asylum seekers' needs and prepare them for the transition to new accommodation.

83. Fieldwork indicates that, for most housing providers, the 14-day period is too short a time to prioritise asylum seekers' needs and prepare them for the transition to new accommodation. Perhaps more importantly, it is difficult to access social security and housing benefits within this timescale. In some cases this is because a significant number of claims are not processed within 14 days; according to recent research, the average elapsed time from the initial housing benefit claim to payment is around seven weeks (Ref. 27). The target for job seekers allowance (JSA), which most successful asylum seekers will claim, is 90 per cent within 21 days rather than 14 days, although 95 per cent are progressed within the 21 day target (Ref. 28). For asylum seekers, average delays are often lengthened as they can rarely provide the documentary evidence that councils and the Benefits Agency require to support claims in the first place. A number of fieldwork authorities, for example, reported that the average time taken to secure social security benefits is four to six weeks. The main reason is the delay in obtaining national insurance (NI) numbers, which are now required for income support, jobseekers' allowance and housing benefit claims as part of counter-fraud measures. Although the Benefits Agency has advised that discretionary interim payments could be made three days after a claim for income support or JSA is received, and that new procedures for issuing NI numbers may improve turnaround times, the overall effect of these problems suggests that more than 14 days may be required to move on adult asylum seekers successfully.

Removing unsuccessful applicants

84. Single adult asylum seekers who receive a negative decision have no further entitlement to NASS housing, and providers will be responsible for determining a sensitive procedure for their removal. As NASS withdraws support from such cases after 14 days, providers need to balance concerns for the asylum seekers' welfare against their own financial interests. Clear guidelines for staff who manage evictions could help to achieve this; staff should also ensure that individuals are provided with information about support that they may be able to obtain through the 'hard cases' fund.

Assessing the financial viability of the housing role

85. Once consortia have identified accommodation and providers, they need to consider the financial implications of the housing role within the framework laid down by NASS. Likely expenditure on accommodation and support services will need to be offset by projected income, and account taken of cash flow issues, the way that income will be recharged to consortia partners, the increased management cost of supporting asylum seekers, and the potential need for new community facilities or initiatives.

86. The successful implementation of local housing and support plans will depend in part on whether the Immigration and Nationality Directorate (IND) meets its new targets for processing asylum claims. NASS has advised consortia that asylum seekers will occupy NASS accommodation for 12 months in 2000/01 and 6 months thereafter, and local plans will be developed on that basis. However, if targets for deciding claims are not met, problems will follow. For example, the type of accommodation and support identified by providers for short-term occupancy may prove unsuitable for longer periods – hostel accommodation with full board could institutionalise residents, if used for long periods, and impede successful claimants' eventual transition to independent living. Delays in turning around claims will also make it difficult for providers to know how much move-on accommodation is likely to be required at different times, or when to start preparing existing residents for transition. If applications run at the levels forecast, and existing stock is full, accommodation plans for each region may need to be amended radically, placing additional pressure on local providers.

87. In an effort to meet its targets, the integrated casework department of the IND has recruited an additional 250 workers to speed up the determination process. In addition, new accelerated procedures for casework were piloted from November 1999; as a result, 63 per cent of new family asylum applications lodged in the first four weeks of November received an initial decision in two months (Ref. 22). However, as there is still an average wait of over a year for an initial decision, further improvements will be needed to achieve the turnaround times forecast for new applications by April 2001. The Government will therefore need to keep the performance of the IND under close review and take prompt action as necessary.

Legal services

88. People who seek asylum are first and foremost making a claim for protection under international law. Legal advice and support is therefore a priority for those who are dispersed by NASS. Asylum seekers may seek support from solicitors or not-for-profit organisations that specialise in immigration law, such as the Immigration Advisory Service and the Refugee Legal Centre. Most applicants supported by NASS will be reliant upon the new Community Legal Service (CLS) Fund (formerly the legal aid scheme) as they will not, by definition, have enough income to pay for legal services.

89. In many areas, the dispersal policy will throw up an imbalance between supply and demand for immigration advice (Ref. 29). A mapping exercise undertaken by the Legal Services Commission to identify immigration law advisers and firms of solicitors contracted to provide immigration services under the CLS Fund in April 2000 found that provision was mainly concentrated in the capital. Of the 423 contracted immigration law firms across England and Wales in April 2000, less than one-half are based outside London [EXHIBIT 10]. While a further 63 not-for-profit organisations have been awarded similar contracts, half of these are also in London. In Wales, only nine firms and four not-for-profit organisations have a Legal Services Commission immigration contract. Almost all are based in Cardiff, and none are based outside South Wales. Moreover, not all immigration contract holders handle asylum cases. While up-to-date information on those handling asylum cases is not available, information from January 2000 showed that just over 90 per cent of all immigration solicitors were undertaking asylum cases; those who do not are more likely to be based outside London. In the short term, this could well undermine the new dispersal policy as, without adequate legal support locally, many asylum seekers may be unwilling to live outside London or other major cities.

90. Although the provision of legal support is not a statutory duty for councils, local authorities can play an important role in addressing shortfalls in their area, possibly through the development of Community Legal Service Partnerships [CASE STUDY 8, overleaf]. In these partnerships, Regional Legal Service Committees of the Legal Services Commission and local authorities work together to assess the need for legal services. If additional services are required, these may be funded jointly by the Legal Services Commission and the local authority. An additional £23 million allocated by the Lord Chancellor in April 2000 will also help to address gaps in legal advice and support on immigration issues and improve the quality of advice for asylum seekers in dispersal areas by funding training on immigration law.

EXHIBIT 10

Map of solicitors' firms and not-for-profit organisations contracted to provide immigration law advice with the Legal Services Commission

Of the 423 contracted immigration law firms across England and Wales, less than one-half are based outside London.

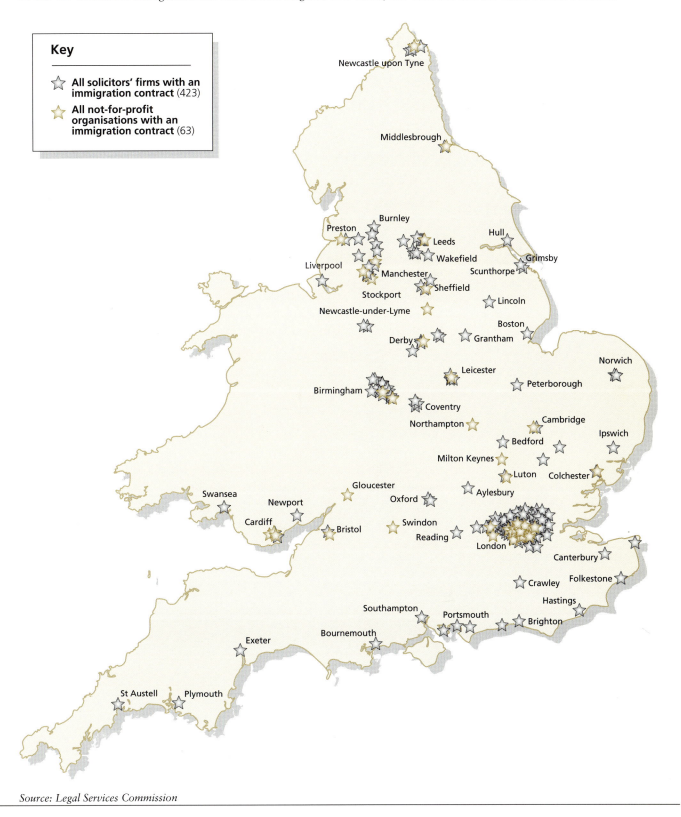

Source: Legal Services Commission

CASE STUDY 8

Developing immigration services through a Community Legal Service Partnership

Liverpool has only two immigration law firms; both have a contract with the Legal Services Commission (LSC), though one is not a specialist in asylum law. Voluntary sector provision is available from the Immigration Advisory Service which is working in collaboration with the Toxteth Citizens' Advice Bureau. The rise in asylum seekers that accompanied voluntary dispersal to the area has meant that the few existing providers are struggling to cope with the increase in casework. There is growing concern that the pressure on existing services will increase if Liverpool has to provide legal support to other asylum seekers who are dispersed to the North West region from April 2000 onwards.

As one of the six pioneer councils involved in developing Community Legal Service Partnerships, Liverpool City Council is already working with the regional committee of the LSC to identify local needs for, and gaps in, legal advice services. The Council currently provides around £1.5 million of grant funding to various advice agencies, including nine Citizens' Advice Bureaux (CABx), several community organisations and two law centres. A corporate grant aid strategy is being developed to ensure that funding is targeted at areas and groups in greatest need.

Through the Community Legal Service Partnership, the council has identified immigration law advice as one area requiring additional funding; with the LSC, it is reviewing how to increase local funding for immigration work. Some £30,000 of council funds, together with at least as much from the LSC, is earmarked to fund up to three posts – those not-for-profit organisations that meet quality mark standards will be encouraged to provide this service. The LSC has also secured additional funds to support further work with asylum seekers and refugees.

Source: Audit Commission fieldwork

91. Although NASS funds the travel costs when asylum seekers have to attend interviews and appeals at the IND offices in Croydon, consortia need to consider whether they should meet the travel costs of those who have to go outside the area for legal advice. These costs are not currently covered by NASS or the Legal Services Commission, although the LSC is considering making some funds available for lawyers and clients who have to travel to provide or obtain immigration advice. Additional costs may also arise when asylum seekers have to attend interviews and appeals; although NASS funds the actual travel costs, who pays for an overnight stay if one is required? Consortia will need to establish financial systems to approve and issue payments for such costs to recipients quickly. If more IND immigration interviews were held locally, overall travel costs could be reduced. In some cases, interviews have been held in regional offices and there is a strong argument for IND to extend this practice.

Health services

92. Although most new arrivals are young and physically fit, a significant number experience health problems that may be linked to the circumstances of their flight – war, torture, rape, witnessing atrocities, loss of family and friends, or the conditions in refugee camps. These are manifest both in physical conditions, such as war or torture injuries, and mental health problems, including post-traumatic stress disorder. Some may also have health problems that are specifically linked to their country of origin or socio-economic circumstances, including HIV/AIDS, poor nutrition or communicable diseases, such as tuberculosis.

93. Asylum seekers, those with ELR and refugees have the same eligibility for NHS-provided healthcare as any other UK resident, and yet many experience difficulty in getting access to health services. The problems often begin with inadequate health assessment at the point of entry to the UK, and continue with problems in accessing primary care services and specialist support, especially mental health services. Barriers to accessing services include the low priority of this group within health authority plans, asylum seekers' lack of knowledge about the UK health system, language difficulties, low awareness among NHS practitioners and NHS bureaucracy [BOX L, overleaf]. Appropriate healthcare services are an important part of the dispersal 'package', and health authorities will need to take steps at a local level to:

- improve the quality of initial health assessments;
- ensure that asylum seekers have access to primary care;
- offer an adequate response to mental health issues; and
- promote access to specialist services for survivors of torture and organised violence.

...the health needs of new arrivals are often not assessed in a systematic way.

BOX L

Bureaucracy as a barrier to healthcare services

Asylum seekers are entitled to free prescriptions or dental treatment on the same basis as any other resident who has received an NHS prescription or been accepted for NHS dental treatment. For example, children under 16 (under 19 if in full-time education), people over 60 or those holding an exemption certificate on maternity or medical grounds are entitled to free prescriptions and sign the back of the form to say why they do not have to pay. Those entitled to free dental treatment (for example, those under 18 or pregnant), tell their dentist why they do not have to pay.

Prior to the introduction of the NASS support arrangements, all asylum seekers who had to pay could apply for help with health costs (NHS charges for prescriptions and dental treatment, optical and hospital travel costs) on the grounds of low income by completing an HC1 form. Those entitled to full help were given an NHS charges certificate, HC2, to obtain free services.

The Commission's fieldwork identified a lack of knowledge about the HC1 process both among health professionals and asylum seekers. The HC1 form is 16 pages long and available only in English, making it difficult for asylum seekers to complete. The forms are not routinely available at GPs' surgeries and asylum seekers may not know how to obtain a form. Delays in processing forms have also presented a barrier to healthcare. In one fieldwork site, an asylum seeker had suffered from severe toothache; he could not afford treatment and was in pain for several weeks before the HC2 certificate arrived.

To improve current arrangements, asylum seekers supported by NASS will be given an HC2 certificate; those not supported by NASS will continue to complete HC1 forms to obtain an HC2 certificate. The Health Benefits Division (HBD), which processes HC1 forms, has recently introduced a fast-track system that seeks to identify asylum seekers' claims for support through the use of a separate HBD postcode. Since December 1999, the HBD has fast-tracked over 1,000 claims from asylum seekers, generally within five working days. Some delays continue to arise, however, when officers in authorities sign the form on behalf of asylum seekers; forms then have to be returned for the applicant's own signature.

Source: Audit Commission fieldwork

Improving the quality of initial health assessments

94. An initial assessment at the point of arrival is an opportunity to explain health services to new arrivals and to start a continuing process of NHS support for those who need health services. It is also a means of identifying communicable diseases, such as tuberculosis, in order to minimise risks to the wider community. While the prevalence of such diseases among new arrivals is low, early detection to prevent any further cases is cost effective. For example, the cost of treating one case of multi-drug resistant tuberculosis (TB) has recently been estimated at approximately £60,000 (Ref. 30).

95. Despite these benefits, the health needs of new arrivals are often not assessed in a systematic way. Those claiming port of entry asylum at Heathrow and Gatwick may, if they are from countries assessed by the World Health Organisation (WHO) as 'high risk', be referred to a Port Health Control Unit (PHCU). These units see some 25 per cent of new asylum seekers each year and have medical officers present 24 hours a day. The process usually involves screening for TB, but medical examinations are often cursory. Follow-up procedures are also poor – there are often practical problems in making further contact with such a highly mobile group, and there is no consistent tracking of those who are screened on arrival. For example, Liverpool Health Authority reported that it receives no information on asylum seekers from Port Health Control, and TB screening has to be repeated. Those who apply in-country, those not considered 'high risk', or those who arrive at a port without PHCU facilities may well receive no health assessment at all.

96. A number of improvements could be made to strengthen initial health assessments. First, better follow-up procedures are clearly equired for passing on information from PHCUs to asylum seekers' eventual area of residence. One option would be to issue medical records to those assessed at the port of entry that asylum seekers could carry and pass on to local service providers. NASS should also inform receiving health authorities of asylum seekers dispersed to their area. Secondly, a more in-depth assessment could be carried out on arrival in a new health district. The Kosovan Humanitarian Evacuation Programme, for example, demonstrated how initial health screening could work more effectively. Leeds and Liverpool Health Authorities used questionnaire-based assessments, administered by interpreters, that covered past medical history and the psychological impact of events in Kosovo. Although there were no reports of any major communicable diseases, new arrivals were offered a test to identify possible cases of TB. The follow-up process included referrals to primary and secondary care, immunisation, addressed sexual health needs and established an appropriate medical record system. Within the first few days of arrival, nearly all (98 per cent) of Kosovan evacuees were registered with GPs in Liverpool.

Ensuring access to primary care

97. Access to good-quality primary care is generally dependent upon registration with a local GP. However, getting access to, and care from, GPs can be difficult. Difficulties sometimes stem from the increased demands that asylum seekers as a group can place on local practices, none of which are reflected in GPs' capitation fees. Language barriers increase the time needed for consultations, and communication difficulties can arise if interpreters are not available [BOX M]. Some GPs advised the Commission that asylum seekers' consultations took on average three to four times longer than those for other patients. The complexity of social problems experienced by asylum seekers, together with their low awareness of what services GPs can provide and how they are delivered, impose further demands on practice resources. Increased administrative work is also an issue with these clients, for example, the typically high mobility of asylum seekers often makes continuity of care more difficult in following up child immunisations, vaccinations and cervical screening and creates work in chasing records. Lack of knowledge about the special needs of the group can also make some GPs reluctant to accept asylum seekers as patients; one recent study reported that many feel uncomfortable when dealing with refugee patients because of concerns that they will be faced with overwhelming need and insurmountable language barriers (Ref. 31).

98. As a result of these issues, some practices have closed their lists to asylum seekers, limiting access to healthcare to a small number of practices that then bear an unfair share of the work. Fieldwork confirmed this pattern of varying willingness to register asylum seekers. Where access is given, practices often prefer to register asylum seekers on a temporary basis, perhaps to minimise the impact on their targets for immunisations and cervical smears and related payments, or because GPs regard their address as 'temporary' even though they do not have a permanent address elsewhere. However, temporary registration also means that medical records are not kept and continuity of care may suffer. Nor does it require a comprehensive new patient health check, as normally happens with a new registration. A recent survey of 56 GP practices in London found that many did not offer a new patient health check to asylum seekers and refugees (Ref. 32).

99. To improve access to primary care, health authorities can set up Local Development Schemes which allow GPs to devote time and resources to asylum seekers [BOX N]. Authorities with such schemes in place provide a model for others to follow and some authorities have already run schemes to provide financial incentives to GPs. For example, Westway Primary Care Group in Kensington, Chelsea and Westminster Health Authority has increased annual capitation payments by £20 for each asylum seeker or refugee. Health Action Zones in England – or Health Alliances in Wales – could also consider the development of specialist services to support this client group.

BOX M

Problems associated with misdiagnosis

A Latin American woman visited her GP to find out about pre-natal care when she was three months pregnant. No interpreter was arranged and she spoke very little English. Because of communication difficulties, the doctor thought that she did not want her baby and arranged a termination; the mistake was discovered only when she went into hospital. In another similar case, the mistake was not discovered and the termination went ahead.

Source: Refugee Council (Ref. 16)

BOX N

Local development schemes for asylum seekers and refugees

Section 36 of the 1997 Primary Care Act gives health authorities the flexibility to improve the development and responsiveness of General Medical Services by giving local GPs financial incentives beyond those set out in the Statement of Fees and Allowances. Local development schemes (LDSs) are funded from health authorities' overall budgets. In 1999/2000, the DoH expected health authorities to spend £5 million on such schemes, out of an additional £60 million that was allocated for GPs' remuneration. Asylum seekers and refugees are one of five suggested target groups for LDSs, and a 'model' scheme developed by the DoH suggests that the following services could be provided to this group in return for enhanced fees:

- *A period of time set aside with a sympathetic member of the receptionist team, preferably in the presence of a link worker or interpreter, to enable registration to be completed outside the clinical process.*

- *A comprehensive mental and physical assessment to identify any serious ongoing problems, and the physical or mental effects of ill-treatment. Such an assessment would usually require the presence of an interpreter and allow a baseline medical record to be developed. The practitioner could also start to inform and educate the patient about the optimal use of primary and secondary care in the UK.*

- *Arrangements to integrate individual asylum seekers and their specific needs into the practice's health promotion programme, to make repeat appointments and, if necessary, re-appointments to enable uptake of preventative procedures such as immunisation and cervical cytology.*

- *Asylum seekers could meet other members of the primary healthcare team to learn about their role in the provision of advice and simple medical treatment or nursing care. Administrative staff would explain ways of obtaining these services from the practice and also provide advice on accessing help for such matters as housing and benefits.*

- *Practitioners could publicise arrangements for referring patients who have been tortured to specialist agencies, and ensure access to language and link-worker support within their practices.*

- *Continued facilitation of access to NHS services would include informing patients of the nature and sites of availability of dental services, and the appropriate use of Accident and Emergency and hospital referral.*

Source: Audit Commission based on information from the Department of Health (Ref. 33)

100. Another way of reducing the strain on a handful of GPs is to establish a dedicated resource for high-mobility groups [CASE STUDY 9]. South Camden Primary Care Group used part of its staff budget to employ a salaried doctor for a year to work in a practice with a high intake of transient patients; the practice has an open registration policy, and takes patients from named hostels. One doctor has overall responsibility for organising care for transient patients and promoting better access to services. This model can work well in an area where there is a high density of refugees, but other areas have found that local practices use GPs with a refugee remit to offload their own asylum-seeking and refugee patients.

CASE STUDY 9

Parkside Health Trust: Improving primary care for high-mobility groups

Parkside Health Trust in West London set up a Health Support Team (HST), including nurses and advice workers, to improve access to primary healthcare services for people in temporary accommodation – predominantly refugees and asylum seekers – and to ease the burden on GPs. A registration protocol is used to assess health needs prior to registration with a practice, and to collect information that practices will need for the new patient registration process. The assessment record and subsequent care plan, as well as client held records, which patients are encouraged to share with other agencies to promote continuity of care, are bilingual. Initial feedback suggests that this gives a comprehensive and detailed picture of individual health needs, and eases administration for practice staff.

A protocol for nurse prescribing is currently being developed. A practice nurse from a local surgery is seconded to the HST for one day a week to share skills and experience and to increase collaboration. Funding is being sought for a staff training programme. A series of 12 training sessions has been piloted on issues such as working with victims of torture and benefits/entitlements for refugees and asylum seekers. To increase inter-agency collaboration, sessions are open to any agency working with these client groups.

Source: Audit Commission fieldwork

Experiences of war, torture or imprisonment may lead to post-traumatic stress disorder.

Promoting access to mental health services

101. Adequate housing, health, education and employment all have a major impact on the mental well-being of refugees and asylum seekers, as indeed they do for other disadvantaged groups. However, the natural distress that accompanies involuntary migration, combined with the need to cope with a new culture, language barriers and loss of status, means that asylum seekers may have higher than average needs for health services. Many experience continued anxiety while awaiting a decision on their claim; while such distress does not constitute mental illness, the cumulative effect of these factors is a higher rate of mental health problems among asylum seekers. Typical conditions presented to GPs include neuroses, anxiety, depression, and phobias (Ref. 34). Experiences of war, torture or imprisonment may also lead to post-traumatic stress disorder.

102. Asylum seekers therefore need both appropriate treatment in primary care, for conditions such as depression or anxiety, and specialist services for mental health problems following trauma. Several GP practices visited now employ counsellors. Elsewhere, severe cases of post-traumatic stress disorder and depression are neglected because of long waiting lists for mainstream mental health services – the latter are often running at capacity for the whole population and can take on only high-risk cases. Some mental health professionals may also lack the expertise that is needed to deal with people from different cultures, or may be unable to provide specialist post-traumatic stress counselling.

103. Some health authorities are trying to bridge the gap in mainstream provision. Lambeth, Southwark and Lewisham Health Authority makes an annual grant of £37,000 to the Refugee Support Centre to provide bilingual counselling for refugees and asylum seekers who are experiencing severe emotional distress. Referrals are mostly from GPs, other primary care practitioners, social services and voluntary organisations. A similar project in North Kensington and North Westminster provides help in accessing mental health services, counselling – including post-traumatic stress counselling – and mental health advice. As the mental health problems experienced by refugees and asylum seekers are often best tackled on an inter-agency basis, the project is multidisciplinary; a psychotherapist co-ordinates the clinical and administrative tasks and there are two counsellors, one support worker and an administrator.

Specialist services for survivors of torture and organised violence

104. For asylum seekers and refugees suffering from the physical or mental effects of torture and organised violence, specialist support is offered by the London-based Medical Foundation for the Care of Victims of Torture. Under the Immigration and Asylum Act 1999, people who are assessed as in need of these services have to be accommodated near London, and their travel costs in attending appointments must be met. Consortia, therefore, need to identify those asylum seekers who fall into this category during initial assessments and make arrangements to pay their travel expenses. Where asylum seekers become clients of the Foundation after dispersal, consortia will have to arrange the relocation of those who wish to move closer to London.

Social services support for unaccompanied minors

105. Under the new legislation, unaccompanied children will not be supported by NASS; instead, social services departments will continue to have responsibilities to support them under the Children Act 1989. The number of unaccompanied children coming to the UK has increased in recent years, from 631 in 1996 to 2,833 in 1998 (Ref. 2). By April 2000, there were over 5,000 unaccompanied children in the care of local authorities. Around 80 per cent of these children were 16 and 17 year-olds and the majority were supported by the London boroughs, with other major concentrations in Kent and West Sussex (Ref. 35).

106. Many unaccompanied children have multiple needs because of their experiences of separation, loss and social dislocation. Their development may be accelerated in some areas and arrested in others, and they may need additional support to make the transition to adulthood. Yet, in many cases, they do not receive the same standard of care routinely afforded to indigenous children in need, even though their legal rights are identical. Many authorities, for example, do not offer 16 and 17 year-old unaccompanied children a full needs assessment, and the Commission's survey found that only one-third had individual care plans in place for all of those in their care. They may also routinely support them in temporary accommodation; survey evidence suggests that over one-half of children over 16, and 12 per cent of those under 16, were in bed and breakfast, hostels and hotel annexes in October 1999. Uncertainty about the age of some claimants sometimes influences the type of accommodation that they are offered. A number of fieldwork authorities reported that an increasing number of young adults are claiming to be under 18 years of age, in order to qualify for additional services under the Children Act 1989. With no reliable way of confirming their age, authorities often place such young people in unsupported accommodation as a matter of course.

Several fieldwork authorities acknowledged that their current arrangements may fail to meet the needs of unaccompanied minors...

107. Several fieldwork authorities acknowledged that their current arrangements may fail to meet the needs of unaccompanied minors, but argue that shortages of suitable accommodation and financial pressures often underlie the low level of support on offer. Many authorities, for example, report increasing difficulty in identifying foster care or residential places for the group, with pressures increasing as demand grows and prices rise. Sometimes this means that children are accommodated outside the boundary of the council supporting them, which can raise problems in supervising their care.

108. Specific government grants are available to meet the costs of supporting this group. In 1998/99, authorities were reimbursed through government grants of up to £200 a week for expenditure on each 16 and 17 year-old and £400 a week for children under 16, subject to a total expenditure limit. In 1999/2000, the 12 local authorities with the largest number of unaccompanied children received £300 per week for 16 and 17 year-olds and £500 for under 16s. The grant regime for other authorities remained unchanged. However, some authorities have struggled to contain costs within the grant thresholds. In 1999/2000, eight local authorities reported average unit costs of over £1,000 per week for children under 16, while the national average was £515 per week. As a result, some authorities have had to 'top up' Government grants. In 1998/99, councils spent almost £4 million over and above the amount reclaimable through government grants. Under the revised grant arrangements for 1999/2000, the estimated shortfall between expenditure and reclaimable grant was still £3 million (Ref. 36).

109. This analysis suggests that an urgent review is required to:

- specify appropriate forms of care for unaccompanied minors;
- agree a standard procedure for age determination; and
- ensure that the grant structure meets the reasonable costs of their support.

In this context, the DoH's recent decision to commission a review of services for unaccompanied children and appropriate models of care is welcome. This should encompass concerns about how those young people still awaiting a decision on their application will be supported when they transfer to NASS support arrangements between the ages of 18 and 21. The transition from care is widely recognised as difficult; those who have already experienced traumatic events may well find it even harder, and a proper care plan to inform that transition is vital. The review might also consider whether the development of central provision could improve standards of care for this group. Small hostels, such as those provided in the early 1980s for Vietnamese unaccompanied children, which were staffed by members of their community and offered proper follow-up support, might usefully be re-visited as models of provision.

Education for school-age children

110. Asylum-seeking and refugee children need access to a wide range of education facilities. Local education authorities (LEAs) expecting to receive asylum-seeking children should, therefore, review various types of support, including early years provision and youth and community services. This section concentrates on schools, since LEAs have a legal duty to ensure that asylum seeking and refugee children aged between 5 and 16 receive appropriate education. It looks at:

- managing school admissions;
- providing additional support services in schools; and
- meeting the costs of educational support.

Managing school admissions

111. Although few authorities visited by the Commission collected information about the number of asylum-seeking or refugee pupils in their schools, or those awaiting admissions, there is some evidence that asylum-seeking children find it difficult to obtain a school place. One London borough had 189 secondary school children waiting for school places – of these, 125 (66 per cent) came from outside the UK, mostly from asylum seekers' countries of origin. Research by the Refugee Council suggests that, in 1999, there were 63,000 refugee children in schools but about 2,000 children had no school place (Ref. 16).

112. Schools with available places cannot legally refuse to admit a child, and the lack of school places for some children may reflect the fact that local schools are full, but there are other reasons why asylum seeking children experience difficulties. Some schools are resistant because they cannot offer the language and other support that the child requires, and/or are concerned that new arrivals will adversely affect GCSE and key stage test results. In some cases, receiving LEAs have been unaware that there were refugee children housed in their area by other councils and have found it hard to keep track of a group with such high mobility. Lack of understanding of educational responsibilities among asylum-seeking parents may also be a factor. For example, a Sierra Leonean woman who could not get places for her children in the school nearest to her home spent the rest of that academic year teaching them at home; she was not aware that any alternative existed.

113. The introduction of the new dispersal arrangements provides an opportunity to address these problems. In future, NASS will be able to inform LEAs of the likely number of children to be placed in their area. Although the children's ages will be impossible to predict, this basic information will allow LEAs to reflect the likely increase in numbers in their school organisation plans. NASS should try to provide as much detail as possible about the children placed in a particular area. LEAs will then be able to monitor admissions more closely and, where necessary, provide targeted support through education welfare officers. Ensuring that school admission and appeal arrangements are clear, fair and objective – and do not disadvantage new arrivals – is also important.

If local schools are full, LEAs should ensure that a suitable place is provided elsewhere, possibly through arrangements with neighbouring LEAs. Better information for parents on the education system, and increasing awareness of the needs of this group among teaching staff and governors, could also help to resolve access problems. Cardiff's Education Department, for example, recently held an asylum seekers conference for local teachers, in partnership with the Refugee Council. A series of practical workshops covered topics such as working with parents in the community and meeting children's psychological and language needs.

114. Even after a school place is found, attendance in schools may be dependent on the availability of other support, such as grants for school uniforms or help to meet certain transport costs. The National Association of Citizens Advice Bureaux cites a number of cases where asylum seekers have struggled to meet the cost of school uniforms. In one case a single parent in London could not meet the estimated cost of £274 for a school uniform and a local Citizens Advice Bureau had to apply to a charity on her behalf. While all asylum-seeking or refugee children qualify for free school meals and milk if it is available, other services remain discretionary. LEAs need to decide whether to provide additional support, taking into account the general availability of these services. If such support is restricted to asylum-seeking children, the rationale for this policy must be justified to the wider population.

Providing additional support in schools

115. Of those asylum-seeking children with a school place, many will need support to thrive in their new environment as a result of their past experiences or current situation. For example, war may have disrupted children's education for several years. Some may have lost relatives or witnessed extreme violence and suffer from emotional and behavioural problems as a result. Once in schools in this country, they may be bullied because of their race or struggle to integrate because of their lack of English. These additional needs place extra pressures on receiving schools and existing specialist education support services. LEAs will therefore have to consider carefully the type of support that they can offer to best meet the needs of these children and of the receiving schools.

116. Schools can assist asylum-seeking pupils to integrate in the classroom in a number of ways; for example, by developing induction programmes and befriending schemes for new pupils, and offering language support and addressing issues of cultural difference through the mainstream curriculum. As their placement can sometimes lead to racial harassment or bullying, schools will also need to ensure that existing policies deal with these problems adequately. Appointing specialist staff, such as refugee support workers and bilingual assistants, can also help new arrivals to integrate. While most of this action will be taken at school level, LEAs should work actively with schools to address the needs of these pupils comprehensively [CASE STUDY 10, overleaf].

Involving the wider refugee and asylum-seeking communities in school life can help to promote the integration of new arrivals.

117. Involving the wider refugee and asylum-seeking communities in school life can help to promote the integration of new arrivals. If schools maintain good communication with parents and carers, problems can often be resolved more quickly. Some schools have adopted imaginative approaches to promote parental involvement, such as inviting them to talk to pupils about their home country or to participate in religious festivals in morning assemblies. Another approach has been to fund local refugee community groups that offer supplementary education to help children to progress in their mainstream schools [CASE STUDY 11].

118. Some LEAs provide additional support to children before they attend schools, or offer different provision as an alternative to a mainstream place. Several LEAs have developed courses for 15–18 year-old pupils whereby they spend a year on an 'access to GCSEs' course, with extensive language support; in others, special reception classes have been set up for younger children to familiarise them with school life. While this type of provision may better equip refugee children to manage in mainstream schools, it is important to weigh the costs and benefits of specialist provision against that provided by mainstream schools. Education professionals report that asylum-seeking children of primary school age often integrate and develop new language skills more quickly by mixing with their local peers.

Meeting the costs of new education support

119. LEAs that previously had few asylum-seeking and refugee children in their schools are likely to lack the infrastructure to support new arrivals. In such cases, LEAs will need to consider what funds can be used to develop new services, especially as the Standard Spending Assessments (SSAs) will not immediately reflect the inclusion of new arrivals. The education SSA formula for 2000/01 in England, for example, is based on the number of primary pupils in local schools at the start of the 1999 spring term, and secondary pupils in schools at the start of the 1999 autumn term.

120. One option open to LEAs in England is to use extra funding from the Standards Fund Ethnic Minority and Traveller Achievement Grant (EMTAG) to develop new services. In Wales, an alternative grant is available under the Grants for Education, Support and Training (GEST) programme. Both funding regimes aim to improve educational achievement in schools among ethnic minorities, including asylum seekers and refugees [BOX O, overleaf]. In 2000/01, EMTAG expenditure is expected to reach £162.5 million, of which over £94 million will be funded by the Government. In Wales, GEST allocations were just over £1.5 million in 1999/2000 and will total £1.85 million in 2000/01.

CASE STUDY 10

Working in partnership to support asylum-seeking and refugee children

In 1998, the London Borough of Camden identified 1,871 asylum–seeking or refugee pupils in its area from 67 countries of origin, forming 9 per cent of the school roll. It drew up policy guidelines to help local schools to support this group. Suggestions included:

- appointing a school co-ordinator to monitor and maintain records of asylum-seeking and refugee children;
- arranging initial assessments to identify asylum-seeking children's needs;
- developing sensitive admissions procedures;
- befriending schemes for new arrivals and phased induction to promote their integration into the mainstream curriculum;
- training staff to increase their awareness of the needs and entitlements of this group;
- making information available in home languages;
- monitoring children's integration into school;
- reviewing the curriculum and school resources to ensure that they reflect the experiences and needs of minority groups and that they counter racism;
- reviewing language policies and providing English language support in mainstream lessons; and
- using the pastoral system to examine bereavement and loss.

Camden LEA has also offered direct assistance to its schools, including:

- translating all standard school letters into other languages;
- providing a standard leaflet that is available in seven languages about educational requirements in the UK for families from other countries;
- information for schools on the education systems in asylum seekers' countries of origin;
- providing in-service training for teachers on refugee issues; and
- developing a directory of mother tongue classes for refugee communities.

Source: Audit Commission fieldwork

CASE STUDY 11

Support through supplementary schools

The Tamil Relief Centre in London has provided supplementary education and training for its community for the last five years. Initially providing classes for 40 children, the Centre now supports over 200 Tamil and other ethnic minority children and has a waiting list for places. Children are helped with their homework and are taught core curriculum subjects, especially maths, English and science. Classes are held after school on weekdays and at weekends. Some children attend from primary school age right through to GCSE years.

Additional tuition is provided for those over 16 to help them with A-level subjects. The organisation believes that this support has increased children's confidence and ability to succeed in school, enabling some to complete their GCSEs and others to go on to universities.

Source: Tamil Relief Centre

BOX O

Ethnic Minority and Traveller Achievement Grant/Grant for Education Support and Training

Ethnic Minority and Traveller Achievement Grant (EMTAG)

The Ethnic Minority Achievement Grant (EMAG) replaced the Home Office-administered Section 11 funding to support ethnic minorities in schools. In 2000/01, EMAG has been merged with an existing Standards Fund grant, used to support Traveller children, to create the Ethnic Minority and Traveller Achievement Grant (EMTAG). This is managed by the Department for Education and Employment (DfEE) and aims to: raise standards of achievement among minority ethnic groups at risk of under-achieving; meet the needs of pupils for whom English is an additional language; and provide support to refugee and Traveller children. Funding may be used for a variety of purposes, including:

- salaries for teachers, classroom assistants, nursery staff and specialist education welfare officers, including bilingual assistants;
- salaries for LEA staff providing in-service training, peripatetic support, monitoring and intervention;
- costs of teaching material and training; and
- other costs specifically related to the education of Travellers and refugees.

The LEA must provide match funding at 42 per cent of the level of central government grant. LEAs can retain 15 per cent of the grant or £150,000 (whichever amount is larger) centrally (excluding the Traveller grant element, which can be retained centrally).

Grant for Education Support and Training (GEST)

The National Assembly for Wales provides funding through its Grants for Education Support and Training (GEST) programme. GEST is used to help schools raise standards and to promote social inclusion; it also provides funds for ethnic minority achievement. The grant is paid at a rate of 70 per cent of expenditure with 30 per cent contribution from the LEA. Welsh LEAs can indicate in their applications how much funding they wish to delegate to schools.

Source: Audit Commission based on information from the Department for Education and Employment and the National Assembly for Wales

121. Some LEAs have successfully used these funds to assist schools to deliver services to asylum-seeking and refugee pupils [CASE STUDY 12]. However, the amount of additional funding likely to be made available to new areas through these programmes will be extremely limited. For example, London and Kent currently receive around 40 per cent of total EMTAG resources and the DfEE has undertaken to protect the cash value of their existing allocations. This is also likely to be the case in Wales, where GEST funds to support ethnic minority achievement have, to date, been largely allocated to just three authorities; in 2000/01, around 92 per cent of funds have been allocated to Swansea, Cardiff and Newport. There will, therefore, be very little available for other areas. Where new funding is allocated to dispersal areas through EMTAG, the requirement to delegate most of the funding to schools could, in turn, make it difficult for LEAs in England to develop any central support structures, particularly if the sum awarded is small. LEAs in both England and Wales may find it difficult to match fund their new allocation, or adapt existing services that are funded by these grants to the needs of a new group. For example, an infrastructure set up to support a well-established Pakistani community in Bradford may not meet the needs of new arrivals from other countries of origin.

CASE STUDY 12

Using EMTAG to support refugee children

The London Borough of Lewisham has 92 schools, many of which regularly receive asylum seekers. In 2000/01, it will receive £2.5 million of EMTAG funding and intends to ringfence £250,000 to support asylum seekers and refugees. The LEA will be adding £50,000 to fund additional needs, of which £20,000 will be allocated to schools, and £30,000 held in contingency to support schools receiving new arrivals during the year. Most of this money will be devolved to between 10 and 15 primary and secondary schools, based on the number of new arrivals in the past year.

Schools use the funding to appoint qualified teachers who provide support for between two and four days a week to asylum seekers. Some also use it to run Family Literacy Projects, providing language support sessions for newly arrived children and their parents or carers. Funding is used to provide crèche facilities and an adult tutor. These projects have been well received by parents and have a waiting list of people who want to attend.

The LEA uses part of the money that is retained centrally to fund a refugee co-ordinator who works three days a week. This post provides support to all new arrivals and to teachers, and visits schools that have no individual refugee support teacher.

Source: Audit Commission fieldwork

*A lack of good written
or spoken English is
a major obstacle to
accessing local services.*

**English language
support**

122. In recognition of these constraints, the DfEE has earmarked an additional £1 million to support asylum-seeking pupils in dispersal areas in 2000/01. If this does not meet the full costs of support, LEAs will have to fund additional support in the short term, supplemented by the resources made available to the consortia and any regeneration or New Opportunities Fund programmes with an education focus that may be running in their areas. They may also need to consider whether existing education services – such as Traveller support teams – could extend their remit to cover new arrivals; Traveller children may, in some cases, share common characteristics with this group. The overall adequacy of local funding will need to be closely monitored by both the DfEE and the National Assembly for Wales; the latter has already suggested that a 100 per cent grant designed solely to meet the additional educational needs of asylum seekers may be preferable to existing arrangements.

123. A lack of good written or spoken English is a major obstacle to accessing local services. It can also prevent both refugees and asylum seekers from participating in the wider community, or from finding work. Special language classes, such as English for Speakers of Other Language (ESOL) courses, run by adult and further education colleges, are commonly used to provide language tuition for refugees and asylum seekers. These courses are often free (or charge low fees) but can be in short supply. In some areas, ESOL courses are heavily over-subscribed; several authorities visited had waiting lists of over 200 people. Consortia need, therefore, to consider how local provision can be developed to meet growing demand.

124. In the absence of a regulatory body to maintain standards, the quality of ESOL provision should be closely monitored. Evidence suggests that courses have not always been rated highly by participants. A study of 236 qualified and skilled refugees in London found that over one-third of those who received language training were dissatisfied with the support that they received; many found the courses too short when their English was very limited at the outset (Ref. 37). Classes may best be provided in partnership with refugee community organisations and may prove most useful to participants if combined with other skills training. Follow-up interviews with service users could help to ensure that future provision better meets the needs of this client group. The National Assembly for Wales has suggested that a national review could also be undertaken to address national variations in both the quality and quantity of ESOL provision.

Employment and training

125. Securing employment is arguably the key factor in the successful integration of refugees in the wider community **[BOX P]**. And historically, many refugee communities have made an important contribution to the UK's economy. The Ugandan Asians who came to the UK in the 1970s, for example, played an important part in revitalising Leicester, where it is estimated that Asian businesses have created at least 30,000 jobs (Ref. 38). Yet although many asylum seekers arrive in the country with professional qualifications from their home countries, and have a high degree of motivation to work, recent research in London reveals that they experience significantly higher levels of unemployment than the population as a whole. One study of 236 qualified and skilled refugees and asylum seekers living in the capital in 1999 found that 42 per cent of refugees and 68 per cent of asylum seekers were unemployed (Ref. 37). Research undertaken by the Home Office has also shown that, for many asylum seekers and refugees, finding employment and getting access to training are their principal areas of concern (Ref. 39).

126. While most asylum seekers have the right to work in a paid or voluntary capacity after six months' residence, both asylum seekers and refugees face major obstacles to employment due to a lack of information about job seeking, the difficulties and expense of re-accreditation for overseas qualifications and experience, language barriers, lack of work experience in Britain and discrimination **[EXHIBIT 11, overleaf]**. Confusion among employers over refugees and asylum seekers' entitlement to work and status has also been cited as an important obstacle to work **[BOX Q, overleaf]**.

BOX P

Integration through vocational training

Victoria came from Sierra Leone in 1997. Like many refugees, she has struggled to overcome extremely traumatic events and rebuild a new life in the UK. On a business administration course, she learned new computer skills and completed a successful work placement. Her achievements on the course were so impressive that in May 1998 she was presented with the Adult Learner of the Year award for South East England, and she now has a full-time job.

Source: Refugee Council

EXHIBIT 11

Barriers to employment

Asylum seekers and refugees have to overcome a number of barriers to employment.

EMPLOYMENT

Racism: racial discrimination may hinder people from getting employment.

Work experience: lack of work experience and a resulting lack of references in the UK may be a disincentive for employers.

Re-accreditation: qualifications from abroad may not be recognised in the UK, requiring people to requalify locally.

National Insurance (NI) numbers: employers may ask for NI numbers. Asylum seekers may have problems obtaining them.

Documentation checks: asylum seekers' papers may say that they are subject to detention and may not say that they have the right to work.

Gender: usually, only principal asylum applicants are granted the right to work. This may exclude many women from the workplace.

Paperwork: asylum seekers must seek permission to work from the IND or have restrictions removed from their documentation.

Status: for the first six months, asylum seekers are normally not entitled to work.

Language barriers: many arrivals speak little or no English. English spoken in other countries may have local differences.

Source: Audit Commission

BOX Q

Restrictions on asylum seekers and refugees in respect to work

Asylum seekers can seek permission from the Home Office to take on paid work after they have been in the country for six months or more. Permission is usually granted only to the main applicant, although dependants can apply and may be granted permission in exceptional circumstances. Notification of permission to work is given in a Home Office letter (GEN 25) or stamped on the reverse of the standard acknowledgement letter

(SAL). The same restrictions apply to voluntary or unpaid work – asylum seekers who undertake such work before they have permission to take on paid work are considered to be 'volunteering illegally' (Ref. 40).

People with refugee status or exceptional leave to remain (ELR) have the right to work in the UK; they do not need to inform or seek permission from the Home Office before taking a job or setting up their own business.

Under Section 8 of the Asylum and Immigration Act 1996, it is a criminal offence to employ anyone who does not have permission to work in the UK. The Refugee Council has voiced concern that this has deterred some employers from recruiting any refugees or asylum seekers. Uncertainty about the length of time people with ELR will remain in the country has also made some employers reluctant to offer this group employment.

Source: Refugee Council

Overcoming barriers to employment and training

127. Home Office asylum statistics show that a significant proportion of asylum seekers will be granted either refugee status or ELR, and it is therefore important that consortia take action to overcome barriers to employment and training, and thus reduce refugees' potential dependency on welfare benefits. Barriers may include: lack of money for transport or suitable clothes to attend interviews; a shortage of affordable childcare provision; and the fragmented nature of local training provision. Many will need guidance on the nature of the job market in the UK, help with interview techniques and pointers as to where to look for jobs. Although many asylum seekers or refugees often choose to re-qualify professionally, this does not always help them to find jobs. In some cases, they may be better advised to build on their skills and experience to pursue new careers, rather than take up courses that lead nowhere.

128. Given these barriers, training providers, advice agencies and other partnerships providing training and employment should strive to:[1]

- use job centres, libraries and local colleges to provide refugees and asylum seekers with information about their entitlements to work (see Appendix 5) and the opportunities available to them, including part-time and evening courses;

- ensure that staff working in local employment and education services are familiar with the training and employment needs of, and opportunities available to, asylum seekers and refugees;

- recognise that refugee community groups are often an important source of information and advice and increase their awareness of education, employment and training opportunities;

- raise awareness among local employers of the employment rights of this group and the range of skills and experience that they offer;

- develop affordable vocational training courses or specialist courses for the accreditation of prior learning and experience;

- promote work placement and work trial schemes with private, voluntary and public sector employers;

- increase refugees and asylum seekers' understanding of the way the jobs market works in the UK; and

- encourage the development of mentoring schemes that link refugees and asylum seekers to people with work experience in the UK.

---

[1] A good source of information on the special training and employment needs of asylum seekers and refugees is the Refugee Education and Training Advisory Service.

...many potential funding regimes are not widely used to support this client group.

Funding new projects

129. While funding attached to NASS housing contracts could be used to address some gaps in provision, consortia should also consider regeneration schemes – such as the Single Regeneration Budget (SRB) programmes or European Social Funds – as feasible sources of funding. A number of regeneration schemes, particularly in London, have used such funds to develop some well-regarded projects for asylum seekers and refugees [CASE STUDIES 13 and 14]. As yet, many potential funding regimes are not widely used to support this client group. The Commission's survey found that, although 50 authorities were running a total of 426 regeneration schemes, only 20 included special projects for asylum seekers and refugees. Private sector sponsorship may also offer additional financial support. During the Kosovan Humanitarian Evacuation Programme, for example, Leeds City Council worked in partnership with Leeds United Football Club to run a successful summer school offering IT and language support for 16 to 20 year-old Kosovan evacuees.

CASE STUDY 13

Developing employment and training projects for asylum seekers through SRB and European funding

In 1997, the London Boroughs of Brent and Harrow, in partnership with the local TEC and five local colleges, set up an agency called Refugees into Jobs. Using a £1.5 million SRB grant and European Social Funds, the agency provides a multi-lingual one-stop information point for local refugees seeking employment and training opportunities. As well as providing careers guidance/support on a casework basis, the agency plays a more strategic role by shaping the provision in local colleges to meet the needs of their clients, developing links with local employers and building the capacity of local refugee community groups. Initiatives developed so far include:

- a Jobs Club, offering clients access to computers, telephones and faxes;

- training in job search skills, including preparing CVs and application forms;

- a grants scheme that helps clients to meet the cost of specialist training courses, books, exam fees, childcare and interview clothes or starting up their own businesses; and;

- a Medical Journal Club to help refugee medical doctors to prepare for their exams.

In 1998/99, 189 of the agency's clients secured interviews for work, of whom 66 were offered jobs. Four volunteers who gained valuable experience by working in the agency also found work.

Source: Audit Commission based on information from Refugees into Jobs

CASE STUDY 14

Re-training refugee doctors

Refugee doctors, although fully qualified in their own countries, are generally unable to practice medicine in this country because their qualifications are not recognised by the General Medical Council (GMC). Before they become eligible for registration, most need to:

- pass the International English Language Testing System examination – the approximate cost for a residential course is £1,000;

- pass a two-stage clinical examination – the Professional Linguistic Assessment Board – which costs £300–£400 for each exam; and

- undertake clinical attachments, which may cost several thousand pounds.

Redbridge and Waltham Forest Health Authority, which had a shortage of 15 GPs in its area, recognised that several local refugee doctors could help to bridge this gap but needed financial assistance to re-qualify. The health authority bid for £610,000 of European regeneration funding over 7 years to support doctors to re-qualify. An additional trust fund, with a remit to improve health and healthcare in the area, has also sponsored additional doctors to go through the process, and local trusts have agreed to co-operate in finding suitable clinical attachments. The average cost per person is £3,500.

Since the scheme was mentioned in the local press, 20 more doctors have signed up. With the cost of training a new medical student estimated at £200,000, this sort of scheme could clearly prove cost effective in the long term.

Source: Audit Commission fieldwork

Tackling documentation problems

130. Some of the problems that asylum seekers face in securing work or training flow from confusion about their entitlements and difficulties in obtaining national insurance (NI) numbers [BOX R, overleaf]. Because the Benefits Agency gives priority to clients applying for benefits when allocating NI numbers, asylum seekers often face lengthy delays in securing them solely for work purposes. Further difficulties arise if local offices require asylum seekers to produce evidence of a job offer or employer before agreeing to interview them for an NI number. Both the National Association of Citizens Advice Bureaux and the Refugee Council have repeatedly identified this as a problem at a local level. Asylum seekers can be trapped in a vicious circle – *they can't get a job because they don't have an NI number and they can't get an NI number because they haven't got a job.*

BOX R

Problems associated with national insurance (NI) numbers

A Zairean asylum seeker with permission to work obtained a part-time job as a cleaner for a local authority, but sought help from a Citizens Advice Bureau (CAB) in outer London because he had not been paid. The reason he had not been paid was because he had no NI number. The Benefits Agency had refused an NI number without ID and birth certificate, both of which were with the Home Office.

A CAB in the Midlands reported the case of a Kosovan asylum seeker with permission to work who could not get an NI number without a job offer. He was asked by all prospective employers for an NI number before they would offer him a job. He had not automatically received an NI number as a result of claiming benefits because he was being maintained under the National Assistance Act.

Source: National Association of Citizens Advice Bureaux (Ref. 17)

131. These problems would be abated if asylum seekers were given a statement clearly setting out their rights and entitlements, or a standard 'permission to work' document by the Home Office. NASS proposals to issue improved documentation to those with refugee status or ELR, may go some way to resolving current problems. Improving the time taken to issue NI numbers, and ensuring that frontline staff have a proper understanding of the rights and entitlements of this group, should be a priority for the Benefits Agency. Where asylum seekers with permission to work receive a final refusal on their claim, the Benefits Agency and Immigration and Nationality Directorate will need to ensure that effective systems are in place to prevent the NI account being used. NASS will also need to give housing providers clear guidance on how asylum seekers' earnings from employment will affect their support, how notification procedures will work and what action will be taken to recover over-payments.

Conclusion

132. Local agencies may face a number of difficulties in providing services to asylum seekers and refugees. These are likely to be more acute in areas with little experience of this client group. Consortia and local agencies will need to consider how any gaps in provision can be addressed and how services can be adapted to meet the short and longer-term needs of new arrivals most effectively. Some local agencies have already had a degree of success in developing new initiatives and can provide a lead for others. However, effectiveness also demands a coherent national framework that offers adequate funding to meet the cost of local services. The role of central government, and its impact on efficiency and effectiveness at a local level, is discussed in the next chapter.

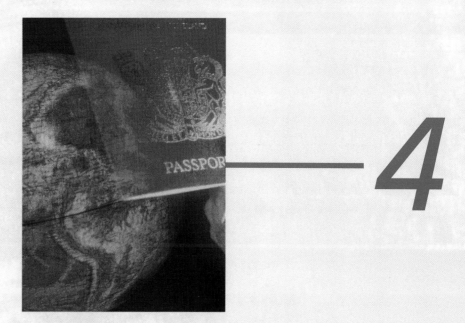

4

Strengthening the National Framework

The efforts of local agencies may not deliver better standards of support for asylum seekers unless there are parallel improvements in the national framework. Turning around asylum applications and appeals more quickly, along with better co-ordinated policy guidance from key government departments, are priorities. A fair and transparent funding regime must also underpin the new arrangements – without this, there is little incentive for local agencies to participate.

133. The increasing number of asylum seekers, combined with frequent changes in the legal framework, have placed immense pressure on local agencies – particularly in London and the south east – and impeded strategic approaches to service delivery. Dispersal and the new support arrangements offer an opportunity to promote a more coherent response to the needs of asylum seekers and refugees, and involve them more in planning local support services. Tailoring support to secure a better match with individual needs, and closer joint working between partner agencies, would also improve current arrangements.

134. The efforts of local authorities and other local agencies may not, however, deliver better standards of support for asylum seekers unless there are parallel improvements in the national framework, and a more effective partnership between central and local government. At a national level, three factors are critical to the success of dispersal:

- making faster decisions on applications and appeals;

- ensuring that the funding regime for asylum seekers meets the reasonable cost of key local services and promotes value for money; and

- improving information-sharing and notification procedures between government departments and local agencies, combined with better co-ordination of national policy.

Making faster decisions on applications and appeals

135. The Government has already recognised that 'delivering faster decisions is crucial to the overall strategy' (Ref. 3). If decisions are not made within the target timescales, it becomes extremely difficult for local agencies to plan an effective response to dispersal. For example, uncertainty about how long new arrivals will remain in NASS accommodation makes it difficult for local agencies to plan move-on accommodation and to prepare people for transition. Slow decisions also have a human cost. Asylum seekers who are left in 'limbo' for long periods of time are at greater risk of marginalisation, with its attendant health and social problems. Higher levels of support will then be necessary to promote the successful integration of those who are allowed to remain in the UK.

136. A number of steps to improve decision making have already been put in place. Extra resources allocated to the Immigration and Nationality Directorate (IND) are being used to recruit more staff, introduce integrated casework procedures and maximise the use of information technology. Considerable progress is already evident – the number of decisions made in the period December 1999 to February 2000 was almost four times greater than in the same quarter in the previous year (Ref. 2). It is vital that this progress is sustained, not least because further improvements are needed to achieve a six-month turnaround of applications by April 2001. At current rates, it would still take over a year

Asylum seekers are a high-needs group and represent new demands on many local budgets...

to clear the backlog even if there were no new arrivals and there are still applicants who have waited over seven years for a decision on their claim.

Deficiencies in the funding framework

137. Adequate funding is crucial to the overall success of the new arrangements. Asylum seekers are a high-needs group and represent new demands on many local budgets, particularly for mainstream education services and healthcare. Many who receive a positive decision will also need extra support to settle successfully and fulfil their potential in this country. The Government's consultation paper on the integration of refugees in the UK, for example, recognises that this group finds 'difficulties in making the transition from support to independence', and that early help will be needed to improve access to services and 'accelerate inclusion into our society' (Ref. 41). Yet if there is no guarantee that the costs of these services and tailored support will be recovered from central government, individual authorities will be reluctant to act as agents for the national scheme. Why agree to accept a high-needs client group that will impose new demands on services and increase the costs for local taxpayers?

138. Prior to the introduction of the new framework, the Government sought to reimburse local expenditure on in-country asylum seekers through specific grant regimes that covered the cost of providing housing and subsistence and the associated administrative overheads.[I] Between April 1999 and December 2000, authorities could reclaim up to £140 per week for adult asylum seekers and £240 per week for families. However, some local authorities have been unable to contain the cost of support for these applicants within these thresholds. Between April and December 1999, authorities spent just over £19 million more than they could reclaim from central government grants or the housing benefit system. London authorities met 92 per cent of this shortfall; in several London authorities 25 per cent or more of their expenditure was not reclaimable under the grant regime [**EXHIBIT 12, overleaf**]. Additional claims from 6 December 1999 up to the end of March 2000 suggest funding shortfalls of a further £10 million for provisions by authorities under the interim scheme. The earlier introduction of voluntary dispersal may have reduced the overall shortfall, by giving London authorities more access to cheaper accommodation elsewhere. As noted earlier, some authorities providing services to unaccompanied minors have also been unable to contain costs within the grant thresholds; in 1999/2000, there was a shortfall of £3 million between the actual and estimated expenditure and the grant thresholds[II] (Ref. 42).

I Port applicants who receive a first negative decision are no longer entitled to benefits and are also supported under this grant regime until they receive a final decision on their claim.

II This calculation is based on actual expenditure up to 28th January 2000 and estimated expenditure up to 31st March 2000.

EXHIBIT 12

Shortfall between total expenditure net of housing benefit and grant reclaimable for adults and families in London, April to December 1999

Between April and December 1999, authorities spent just over £19 million more than they could reclaim from central government grants or through housing benefit. London authorities met 92 per cent of this shortfall.

Shortfall between total expenditure net of housing benefit and grant reclaimable (£m)

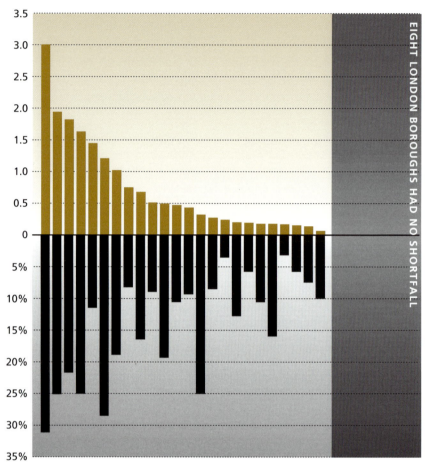

Shortfall as a percentage of total gross expenditure

■ **Difference between total expenditure net of housing benefit and grant reclaimable**

■ **Shortfall as a percentage of total gross expenditure**

Note: Corporation of London is not included.

Source: Audit Commission based on data from the Home Office

139. Analysis of the unit cost of grant-aided provision for housing and support across authorities in England and Wales reveals considerable variation. One authority spends, on average, under £50 per week per family while another spends ten times this amount [**EXHIBIT 13**]. Differing local circumstances – notably rent levels and the capacity to draw upon lower-cost council stock – partially explain these differences. Additionally, costs may vary because of methods of procurement; long-term contracts for accommodation may, for example, be more cost effective than spot purchasing, and include a broader range of services, such as travel costs or English language, in the contract price. Variations in central overhead costs may also account for different levels of expenditure. The Commission's survey found that staff numbers in local asylum teams ranged from 3 to 41, but that there was no clear relationship between the number of staff and the number of asylum seekers supported. Some authorities may therefore be making better use of their resources than others.

EXHIBIT 13

Unit costs for support to asylum-seeking families in England, April to December 1999

Average spending varies by a factor of ten.

Note: 50 out of 122 authorities (41 per cent) providing support had unit costs over the £240 threshold in 1999.

Source: Audit Commission, based on data from the Home Office

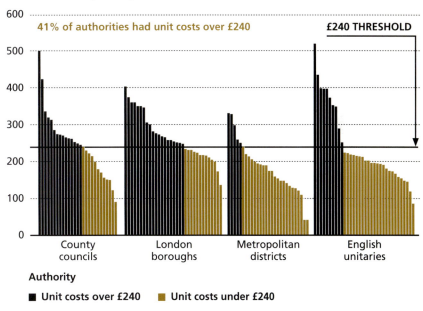

Unit costs under grant regime (£)

41% of authorities had unit costs over £240

£240 THRESHOLD

Authority

■ Unit costs over £240   ■ Unit costs under £240

The Government explicitly recognised the costs of additional support in its separate grant regime for the Kosovan Humanitarian Evacuation Programme but has not done so for other asylum seekers.

140. As the grant regime covers only housing, subsistence and related administration costs for in-country applicants, other costs have fallen on local budgets. For example, asylum seekers who claimed at the port of entry before 3 April 2000 are entitled, if they meet 'priority need' criteria, to housing under homeless legislation. London authorities bore net expenditure costs in excess of £15 million in 1997/98 because thousands of asylum seekers in receipt of housing benefit had to be placed in homeless persons accommodation[1] (Ref. 43). Other service costs, such as education for refugee children and English language support for adults, are met from existing budgets – only some of this expenditure is eventually recouped through the Standard Spending Assessment (SSA) formula. The Government explicitly recognised the costs of additional support in its separate grant regime for the Kosovan Humanitarian Evacuation Programme but has not done so for other asylum seekers. [BOX S]. Unfortunately, few councils or health authorities record their additional expenditure on other services for this client group and so the full level of subsidy that is being met from local budgets is unknown.

141. The funding framework introduced by NASS to support dispersal aims to provide a more realistic basis for meeting the direct local costs of support for asylum seekers. NASS has emphasised that it will negotiate with local authorities/consortia and potential providers have been invited to identify their estimated costs for the following items:

• council rent;

• council tax;

• utilities (gas, water and electricity);

• initial furnishings and utensils (bedding, pots, pans, cutlery, etc.);

• management charge; and

• replacement items.

Providers may be able to include other items – such as English language support and translation and interpretation costs – in their management overheads, subject to NASS agreement. The new funding framework is not, however, designed to meet the statutory healthcare and education costs that will arise through dispersal, although the Home Office funding model does show some illustrative costs (Ref. 45). For example, NASS estimates that the unit cost of education provision for an asylum-seeking family will be £272 per month, while health costs are estimated at

---

I There are a number of reasons why temporary accommodation lettings may generate direct costs that are a net loss to the General Fund. Fixed ceilings for housing benefit (HB) – tied to a multiple of average council dwelling rents – may lie below prevailing private sector rents or room charges, leaving the local authority to find the difference. The loss tends to be largest on bed and breakfast accommodation. Irrecoverable rent arrears, nomination fees for placements in RSL stock and staff/ management overheads may also generate additional costs. Finally, where the tenant claims HB the authority must contribute the standard 5 per cent of its value that central government does not reimburse through HB subsidy.

£96 per month – £4,416 in all for each family annually. For single adults, health costs are estimated at £32 per month, or £384 annually. A key assumption of the model is that for each family dispersed there will be three single adults; if this ratio hold true, total health and education costs will total £5,568 per year for each group of three adults and one family dispersed under the new arrangements.

BOX S

Funding regime for Kosovans under the Humanitarian Evacuation Programme

Subject to a spending threshold, local authorities could reclaim expenditure for the period 1 April 1999 to 31 March 2000 on:

- the costs of airport arrival and departure teams;
- the costs incurred in establishing, preparing and closing down reception centres and return centres;
- volunteer expenses (travel and subsistence);
- the costs of running reception centres;
- the administrative costs incurred in arranging the reception and care of evacuees;
- the costs of establishing and running regional co-ordination teams, the non-capital cost of the assessment and provision of social services;
- the non-capital costs of educating children of school age;
- the costs of providing and furnishing housing or temporary accommodation (subject to an average upper limit of £5,000 per unit of accommodation);
- the costs of interpretation services;
- the costs of English language support and vocational training to cater for the particular needs of Kosovan evacuees, other than children of school age;
- loss of rental income where an authority can provide evidence of the income loss and that this was unavoidable; and
- additional external audit fees.

Source: Audit Commission, based on information from the Home Office (Ref. 44)

142. The model inevitably raises a question about how these additional costs will be met. In the long term, SSAs and health authority allocations should offset some expenditure on education and healthcare. However, these funding mechanisms are not designed to reflect the full cost of providing schooling or primary care to this high needs client group and will not take account of any increase in new arrivals in the short term. Those areas with little existing infrastructure to support asylum seekers may, therefore, find it particularly hard to contain initial set-up and service costs. If this results in inadequate services, long-term costs could be generated, as those asylum seekers who eventually receive ELR or refugee status could well take longer to settle and be at greater risk of marginalisation in the dispersal area. To avoid this, relevant Government departments – including the DfEE, DoH and the Home Office – should ensure that there are sufficient resources available to dispersal areas to meet the cost of statutory services that new arrivals will require. The DfEE has recently recognised that additional costs will arise in dispersal areas and has earmarked an additional £1 million to cover new costs in 2000/01. However, it is unclear how this sum was calculated; compared to the Home Office's projected education costs, it would only provide full year funding for just over 300 asylum-seeking families. In practice, further resources may need to be allocated to meet the actual health and education costs that new arrivals will generate in dispersal areas in the short term.

Promoting value for money and information sharing

Service provision for asylum seekers should be subject to the same value-for-money scrutiny as other services.

143. Service provision for asylum seekers should be subject to the same value-for-money scrutiny as other services. At present, few authorities collect comprehensive information about expenditure on this client group and there is no systematic attempt to monitor performance. Variations in the unit cost of housing and support raise serious concerns about whether value-for-money has been achieved to date under the grant regime.

144. In order to monitor value for money, NASS should collect more information on the comparative costs for services to asylum seekers and their link with performance outcomes. This will require a standard framework for calculating and assessing unit costs, service take-up and effectiveness across each consortium and housing provider under the new support arrangements [BOX Q, overleaf]. This approach would allow both authorities and the Government to compile comparative data sets, benchmark costs and services and set meaningful performance targets. It may also help to identify models of efficient service delivery that could be more widely promoted, and ensure that the overall financial framework is robust. Standard definitions are needed to support whichever cost and performance measures are used. As with all comparative exercises, different local circumstances will need to be taken into account in the evaluation process. Without this type of cost and service quality information, many authorities will struggle to demonstrate the achievement of best value under the Local Government Act 1999.

145. The new arrangements must be underpinned by an effective system for information-sharing and notification procedures between central and local agencies. As the voluntary arrangements for dispersal have demonstrated, a lack of basic background and operational information makes it difficult to provide appropriate accommodation and the right mix of support services. Consortia will struggle to work effectively unless they:

- know the individual profile of new arrivals to be dispersed to their area, including their nationalities, languages spoken, gender, ages and special needs;

- know the length of time applicants are likely to wait for a decision on their claim;

- receive prompt notification of the decisions made on individual cases;

- have details of any additional housing contracts awarded in their area – without this information it is difficult to assess the overall level of new demand that new arrivals will generate and plan their response accordingly; and

- receive early notification of any changes in the Government's asylum procedures or support arrangements.

146. More clarity about how dispersal will be implemented nationally is also required. While the Government has, to date, suggested that asylum seekers will be dispersed on the basis of the languages that they speak, a shortage of suitable housing may increasingly necessitate an accommodation-led approach. If this is the case, consortia plans for service delivery may need to be revised. If a range of different languages is spoken by new arrivals and their profile differs markedly from existing multi-ethnic populations, the need for new services is likely to be greater. Further clarification of other aspects of the support arrangements, such as a clear definition of what is meant by 'essential living needs', is also required. Without a clear definition of what is meant by this term, local providers may adopt different interpretations, leading to wide variations in the costs and standards of support by different consortia.

BOX Q

Assessing the cost, efficiency and effectiveness of support for asylum seekers

The following information on costs, efficiency and performance could be collected to identify how housing providers and consortia are meeting the needs of asylum seekers. These are exemplary ideas only but offer a potential menu of sources for comparative information. Certain issues, such as a satisfaction survey, might best be developed at the national level to allow for meaningful comparison.

Housing providers

- Number of staff (full-time equivalents) involved in housing management per asylum seeker housed.

- Housing rent cost per asylum seeker household (for example, per 1 bed or 3 bed placement).

- Percentage of asylum seekers allocated who stayed in NASS accommodation until a decision was made.

- Average wait per asylum seeker for move-on accommodation after a decision.

- Results of an asylum seekers' satisfaction survey.

Regional consortia

- Performance against a checklist of information to be provided to asylum seekers (for example, map of local area, addresses of local services, details of local shops that accept vouchers).

- Number of frontline staff (full-time equivalents) in regional consortia working with asylum seekers per asylum seeker sent to the region.

- Number of positive local press articles on asylum seekers compared to total number of local articles on asylum seekers/refugees.

- Amount of external funding/sponsorship attracted for projects for asylum seekers/refugees compared to number of asylum seekers in the region allocated by NASS.

- Percentage of asylum seekers registered with a GP within a month of arrival.

- Percentage of asylum seekers receiving a new patient health check within two weeks of registering with a GP.

- Percentage of asylum-seeking children placed in school within a month of arrival.

- Average number of hours of English as an additional language (EAL) support per asylum-seeking child with EAL needs in schools.

BOX Q (cont.)

Assessing the cost, efficiency and effectiveness of support for asylum seekers

- Number of refugee community organisations (RCOs) supported compared to number of asylum seekers allocated by NASS; average grant per RCO.

- Percentage of NASS-supported cases remaining in dispersal area six months after a positive decision.

Source: Audit Commission

Co-ordinating policy across Whitehall

The Government could further assist authorities by ensuring that policy on asylum seekers and refugees is well co-ordinated...

147. The Government could further assist authorities by ensuring that its policy on asylum seekers and refugees is well co-ordinated at a national level, perhaps through a strategic framework designed to meet the needs of this group. Although the new legal framework sets out a range of proposals to reform the asylum process, it would be helpful if the Government made explicit the roles that other government departments – especially the DfEE, DSS and DoH – will play in the new arrangements. And it is puzzling that the Social Exclusion Unit appears so far not to have been represented on the Government's interdepartmental policy forum, given this client group's high risk of marginalisation and exclusion. Clarity around expectations, detailed policy guidance and the responsibilities of each department to make dispersal work and to promote settlement, would be welcomed by all engaged in working with asylum seekers and refugees and would ensure more effective service delivery.

The way forward

148. Providing effective and appropriate services to asylum seekers and refugees represents a significant challenge for local agencies, particularly those with little history of providing support. The current arrangements offer no guarantee that the needs of asylum seekers will be met in a consistent way, due to shortcomings at both the local and national level. These weaknesses can be remedied where local agencies work together through the regional consortia to improve needs analysis, promote a more strategic approach to service delivery and give service users a stronger voice. Government needs to support these efforts by improving the national framework – speeding up the decision-making process on applications and appeals, co-ordinating the policy framework across different departments, and ensuring that the funding mechanisms cover essential local costs and secure value for money [EXHIBIT 14]. Securing improvement will take time, but the potential gains are worth striving for:

- improved standards of service for asylum seekers, helping to ensure that those who remain in the UK can contribute to, and enrich, our national life;

- reduced levels of social exclusion and racial tension;

- the prevention of 'drift back' to London; and

- better use of public money.

EXHIBIT 14

Critical success factors for dispersal: partnership working and better use of resources

Local agencies and national government can work in partnership to improve standards of service to asylum seekers and make better use of resources.

Source: Audit Commission

RECOMMENDATIONS

4 — Another Country

Recommendations for regional consortia and local authorities/agencies

Improving the delivery of services at a local level will involve councils, health agencies, registered social landlords (RSLs) and housing associations, private sector landlords, the police and the voluntary sector, working in partnership through the new regional consortia. Together these agencies will need to:

1 Establish clear managerial and political leadership for regional consortia (paragraphs 31–34).

2 Carry out a strategic review of services, priorities and resources for asylum seekers and refugees, considering how resources can be pooled to develop joint provision (paragraphs 40–45).

3 Identify the needs and profile of all asylum seekers and refugees within the area, ensuring that data is shared between agencies (paragraphs 41–42).

4 Establish information systems to monitor the take-up of services among asylum seekers and refugees, and to identify the costs arising (paragraph 43).

5 Develop a public relations strategy for asylum seekers and joint procedures for communicating with the media (paragraphs 49–50).

6 Promote sensitive policing policies to ease community tensions (paragraph 52).

7 Review accessibility of services to asylum seekers, and improve access where problems are apparent (for example, through better signposting, staff training, interpretation, translation and advocacy services) (paragraphs 53–61).

8 Develop effective consultation mechanisms to involve asylum seekers and refugees and their community groups in service planning (paragraphs 63–64).

9 Promote the development of refugee community organisations and ensure that local grant criteria address the needs of this group (paragraphs 65–67).

10 Consider whether existing regeneration programmes, National Lottery funding or private sector sponsorship could provide additional resources for dedicated services for asylum seekers or refugees (paragraphs 67, 129).

RECOMMENDATIONS

4 Another Country

Recommendations for government departments

Improving the national framework falls mostly within the remit of the Home Office, with the Department of Health (DoH), the Department of Social Security (DSS), and the Department for Education and Employment (DfEE) contributing on specific aspects.

11 The Home Office should establish protocols for information sharing and notification procedures between government departments, and from government departments to local agencies (paragraphs 38–39).

12 The DoH and DfEE should issue good practice guidance to local health authorities and education authorities respectively to ensure effective service delivery to asylum seekers and refugees (paragraphs 38–39).

13 NASS should ensure that national information on asylum seekers is shared with consortia and other local agencies to inform service planning (paragraph 43).

14 The DoH/NASS should issue new arrivals with information about their entitlement to health services and a simple explanation of how the UK health system operates (paragraph 55).

15 The Home Office/DfEE should consider whether restrictions on all/specific types of voluntary activity for asylum seekers should be lifted (paragraph 59).

16 The IND should issue standard documentation to new arrivals at each port of entry and consider introducing a 'rights statement' that asylum seekers can carry with them that sets out their entitlements to services (paragraph 62).

17 NASS should provide each consortium with details of other housing providers that are contracted to provide accommodation in their area (paragraphs 71, 144).

18 The Home Office/DSS should review the decision to terminate accommodation and support for adult asylum seekers 14 days after a positive decision on their asylum claim (paragraph 83).

19 The IND should seek to expand the practice of holding immigration interviews in regional offices in order to reduce travel costs (paragraph 91).

RECOMMENDATIONS

4 Another Country

20 Port Health Control Units should issue medical records to those screened at ports of entry that can be used to inform other health service providers (paragraph 96).

21 The DoH/Home Office should review the funding framework for support for unaccompanied minors and issue best practice guidance to local authorities on providing services to this group (paragraphs 105–108).

22 The DSS should issue guidance to standardise practice across local Benefits Agencies on the allocation of national insurance numbers to asylum seekers and refugees (paragraphs 130–131).

23 The Home Office, DfEE and the DoH should ensure that there are sufficient resources available to dispersal areas to meet the reasonable cost of statutory services for asylum seekers (paragraphs 137–142).

24 NASS should collect more information on the comparative costs of services to asylum seekers and their links to performance outcomes (paragraphs 143-144).

25 The Home Office should ensure that government policy on asylum seekers and refugees is better co-ordinated at a national level, perhaps through a national strategic framework that is designed to meet the needs of this group (paragraph 147).

Appendix 1

Advisory group

Eid Ali Ahmed	Liaison Officer, Asylum and Refugee Issues, Equality and Policy Unit, National Assembly for Wales
Terrie Alafat	Director of Housing and Strategic Development, Royal Borough of Kensington and Chelsea
David Barnes	Project Manager, West Midlands Asylum Seekers Consortium
Dermot Boyle	Chief Executive, Refugee Arrivals Project
Mike Boyle	Head of Asylum Team Project, Local Government Association (LGA)
Mark Brangwyn	Social Policy Officer, Association of London Government
Simon Dow	Deputy Chief Executive, Housing Corporation
Alison Fenney	National Development and Policy Team Manager, Refugee Council
Fahmeeda Gill	Policy Officer, National Housing Federation
Andy Gregg	Director, Refugee Education and Training Advisory Service
Janet Haddington	Manager, Asylum Team, Westminster City Council, and London Asylum Seekers' Consortium
Alison Harvey	Advocacy Officer, Medical Foundation for the Care of Victims of Torture
Caroline Lowdell	Policy Analyst, The Health of Londoners' Project
Ann Mercer	Section Head, Social Care Region 2, Social Services Inspectorate
Susan Rowlands	Director, Immigration Law Practitioners Association
Judith Simpson	Head of Support Provision, National Asylum Support Service, Home Office
Sandra Skeete	Director, Refugee Housing Association
Penny Thompson	Director of Social Services, Sheffield City Council

Appendix 2

Refugee community panel

Mr Alemayehu	Ethiopian Community in Britain
Afzal Mirza	Refugee Advice Centre
Joe N'Danga Koroma	Association of Sierra Leonean Refugees
Sarah Nansukusa	Ugandan Community Relief Association
Lizzette Robleto	Latin American Women's Rights Service
Mr Gevara Tali	Albanian Community in the UK
Mr Thangaraja	Tamil Relief Centre

Appendix 3

Summary of the Immigration and Asylum Act 1999

The Immigration and Asylum Act 1999 (Ref. 20) is a substantial piece of legislation with 138 separate clauses and 14 schedules, touching upon almost every aspect of the asylum and immigration system in the UK.

Part I introduces new immigration controls, including powers to give or refuse leave to enter prior to arrival in the UK and to charge fees for applications. It introduces powers to require financial 'security' for the grant of entry clearance and extensions of stay and creates new criminal offences if, by using 'deception', a person obtains or seeks to obtain leave to enter or remain in the UK.

Part II extends carriers' liability fines to cover all road passenger vehicles, shipping, air transport and international rail services. A new civil penalty is aimed at carriers bringing clandestine entrants into the UK. There are new powers to impound and sell vehicles if penalties are not paid. A code of practice is introduced for employers checking documentation and employment restrictions under the Asylum and Immigration Act 1996.

Part III considers detention and provides for detainees to be given 'routine bail hearings' after one and five weeks, to be heard by magistrates' courts or special adjudicators, or by television links from detention centres. A new offence is introduced for resisting or obstructing a custody officer.

Part IV addresses appeals. The Immigration Appeal Tribunal (IAT) is maintained but appellants can raise breaches of human rights as part of the appeal in a 'one-stop' procedure. Rights of appeal for overstayers are largely removed. A new power is introduced to impose financial penalties for individuals pursuing appeals to the IAT without merit. The 'white list' of 'safe' countries is abolished – but asylum certification (immediate refusal and limited appeal rights) will remain in some cases.

Part V establishes an Immigration Services Commissioner to regulate immigration advice and to set standards for the profession. It requires advisers to pay a fee to register, though some providers may be exempt. A new offence is introduced for non-registered advisers. An Immigration Services Tribunal is introduced to hear cases against unscrupulous advisers. The Commissioner will have powers to enter and search premises and seize documents.

Part VI introduces new support provisions. All new asylum seekers (except unaccompanied minors) will be excluded from benefits, housing and, where need is based solely on destitution, provision under the National Assistance Act 1948 or Children Act 1989. Instead they will be supported by a new Home Office National Asylum Support Service (NASS). NASS will allocate accommodation to destitute asylum seekers and will provide subsistence, largely in the form of vouchers rather than cash benefits.

Part VII extends immigration officers' powers of entry, search and arrest. Some of these powers will not require a warrant. Officers may use 'reasonable force' to carry out their duties, giving them broader powers than the police in some circumstances.

Part VIII addresses immigration detention centres. It makes provision for the operation and management of these centres, including those that have been contracted-out, and sets out the functions of detention centre managers.

Part IX clamps down on the abuse of civil marriages. It imposes a duty on civil marriage registrars to report any marriage to the IND if they suspect that its purpose is to 'evade immigration control'.

Appendix 4

Sources of national and local data on asylum seekers and refugees in the UK

TYPE OF DATA	SOURCE	INFORMATION PROVIDED	CAVEATS
National asylum seeker data	Home Office, IND	Figures on asylum applications and decisions by nationality are available in annual/ monthly bulletins.	Not broken down by region/local authority area.
	Home Office, NASS	A database on asylum seekers and refugees, with information on individual applicants supported by NASS, will be developed shortly.	To date, not all information is computerised. It will only include details of applicants supported by NASS.
Income support data	Department of Social Security	Information on Income Support (IS) claimants – refugees and asylum seekers are included in a category with other urgent case payment recipients.	Figures are only a subset of refugees and asylum seekers, as they only include data on those in receipt of IS. Asylum seekers and refugees are not separated from other cases.
New registrations with GPs	GPs/health authorities	GPs should complete a form for new migrants, including asylum seekers, who register.	Figures only count those who register; coding is inconsistent and may be incomplete; data may be difficult to access.
Ethnic group classifications of hospital in-patients	Hospitals/health authorities	In theory, all hospital in-patient records should have an ethnic group coding.	Recording of ethnic group varies. Refugees and asylum seekers are only a subset of ethnic groups. Only covers hospital admissions.
Refugee children in schools	Schools/local education authorities (LEAs)/ Refugee Council	Schools and LEAs may collate information but this is not gathered centrally – the Refugee Council has published estimates from data available.	Not all schools/LEAs collect this information. Coding by schools varies, and estimates are based on different methodologies.
Language(s) spoken in schools	Schools/LEAs/ School of Oriental and African Studies (SOAS)	Many schools collect data on languages spoken in schools – sometimes this is collated centrally and published by LEAs. The University of London's School of Oriental and African Studies has collated London data.	Data is of languages which does not denote if speakers are asylum seekers or refugees. Covers children, not the whole population.
Arrivals data	Refugee Arrivals Project (RAP)	Based at Heathrow and Gatwick airports, RAP has information on where arrivals at these ports of entry are assigned on arrival.	Applies only to two ports of entry (estimated to cover one-third of port asylum seekers). Project aims to spread allocations therefore data may not reflect the location of asylum seekers and refugees as a whole.

TYPE OF DATA	SOURCE	INFORMATION PROVIDED	CAVEATS
Port 101H forms	Health Control Units (HCUs) at air and sea ports	HCUs at airports see people referred by immigration control – mainly those seeking to stay in the country for at least 6 months, including most asylum seekers – details are passed on to health authorities and sometimes environmental health departments in local authorities where people first intend to live.	Not all terminals are computerised, limiting the data available. Not all asylum seekers apply at port of entry (currently only about one-half). People may not stay at the given address and information may not reach the relevant area where the asylum seeker ends up.
Bed and Breakfast Information Exchange (BABIE)	London Research Centre	Data on the number of asylum seeker homeless households in temporary accommodation in London local authorities.	Only covers London. Only records a subset of asylum seekers. Information is not collected by country of origin.
Registration data	Office for National Statistics	Country of birth information on registration forms of births and deaths.	Country of birth not refugee status is recorded. Published data are for broad regions and not individual countries.
Mid-year population estimates	Office for National Statistics	Each year an estimate is made of the additional number of asylum seekers and people who change status in the UK. This is added to government's official population estimates for each area.	National figures from the Home Office are allocated to boroughs using 1991 Census country of birth distributions, not actual refugee distributions. Census data is used by broad regions.
Community group cases	Local community organisations	Voluntary groups working with refugees/ asylum seekers will have figures on their caseloads.	Figures will not cover the whole community. Figures will not be comparable between different areas.
2001 census country of birth data	Office for National Statistics	In 2001 the census will require all residents to record their country of birth – this could cover all countries if they are all coded.	Identifies migrants not refugees. Data will not be available until 2003.
Police registration	Police forces	Until March 1998 people granted refugee status or exceptional leave to remain (ELR) who were not nationals of a Commonwealth or European Economic Area country had to register with police.	Identifies a subset of refugees only. Does not identify those not granted refugee status or ELR, but still in the country.

Appendix 5

Main welfare entitlements and support for asylum seekers, refugees and people with ELR at 3 April 2000

SERVICES	PORT ASYLUM SEEKER PRE 3 APRIL 2000	IN-COUNTRY ASYLUM SEEKER/ PERSON AWAITING APPEAL	NEW ASYLUM SEEKER FROM 3 APRIL 2000	PERSON WITH EXCEPTIONAL LEAVE TO ENTER OR REMAIN (ELE/ELR)	PERSON WITH REFUGEE STATUS
National Health Service/GP services	Yes	Yes	Yes	Yes	Yes
Early years school provision	Yes	Yes	Yes	Yes	Yes
School provision 5–16	Yes	Yes	Yes	Yes	Yes
Further education (eg, college)	Overseas student rates in theory, but concessionary fees may be offered for part-time students on welfare benefits or vouchers			Same as home student – fees may apply	Same as home student – fees may apply
Higher education grants (eg, university)	No	No	No	After 3 years	Yes
Higher education fees	Overseas student rate – liable for full fees			Same as home student	Same as home student
Welfare benefits/ NASS support[I]	90% of Income Support, 100% housing and council tax benefit	Vouchers and £10 cash for single people and couples; cash support for families under Children Act	Vouchers and £10 cash per person per week [II]	Yes	Yes
Social housing	Temporary via homelessness legislation if in priority need	Temporary via statutory interim arrangements or the Children Act	NASS accommodation for destitute port applicants with no other means of support [II]	Yes	Yes
Social services (eg, community care)	Yes	Yes	Yes, but with exceptions [III]	Yes	Yes

I   There are some exceptions to the general rules listed in the table. Port applicants on appeal who have 'temporary admission' may retain entitlement to housing/council tax benefit. Other asylum seekers (port/in-country) may have these entitlements, plus access to social housing on the basis of their nationality or country of origin.

II   From 3 April 2000, port applicants will be eligible for NASS support subject to certain criteria testing for destitution. In-country applicants will continue to be supported by local authorities until their phased entry into the NASS scheme.

III   Asylum seekers will be excluded from the Children Act 1989 and community care legislation, where need is based solely on destitution. All other aspects of this legislation will apply to asylum seekers and their dependants (eg, regarding child protection).

References

1. Speech by Rabbi Hugo Gryn, 'A moral and spiritual index', The Refugee Council/ Jewish Council for Racial Equality, 1997.

2. Home Office, *Statistical Bulletin: Asylum Statistics UK 1998*, Government Statistical Service, 27 May 1999, plus additional asylum statistics for 1999 and 2000, available from Home Office Research, Development and Statistics Directorate.

3. *Fairer, Faster and Firmer: A Modern Approach to Immigration and Asylum*, cm 4018, HMSO, 27 July 1998.

4. Asylum Rights Campaign (ARC), *Out of Sight: Out of Mind*, ARC, London, 1999.

5. *Hansard*, House of Commons, oral answers, 10th April 2000, column 12.

6. *Hansard*, House of Commons, written answers, 6th April 2000, column 591.

7. Health of Londoners Project, *Refugee Health in London: Key Issues for Public Health*, Health of Londoners Project, June 1999.

8. Immigration and Nationality Directorate (IND), *Cluster Areas*, IND, Home Office, February 2000.

9. Immigration and Nationality Directorate, (IND), 'Process Manual for the Asylum Support System', (first draft), IND, Home Office, 17 February 1999.

10. National Asylum Support Service (NASS), 'Phased Introduction of the Support Arrangements', 24 March 2000.

11. Local Government Association, (LGA), *Asylum Seekers Voluntary Dispersal Scheme, Bulletin No. 5*, LGA, week ending 11 February 2000.

12. Figures provided by the London Asylum Seekers Consortium (LASC), 'Breakdown of referrals received and placed by London boroughs for period 2 July 1999 to 7 January 2000', January 2000.

13. Home Office, National Asylum Support Service, (NASS), *Draft Memorandum of Understanding: the Development of a Commissioning Strategy and Creation of an Enabling Function by Consortium, Financial Year 1999/2000*, NASS, November 1999.

14. Audit Commission, *A Fruitful Partnership: Effective Partnership Working*, Audit Commission, London, 1999.

15. British Medical Association (BMA), Letter to IND, 'Home Office Consultation Paper on the Integration of Recognised Refugees in the UK: Response of the British Medical Association', 13 December 1999.

16. Refugee Council, *Information Service: The Information Survivor Kit for Public and Voluntary Sector Employees*, Refugee Council, December 1999.

17.   National Association of Citizens Advice Bureaux, (NACAB), *A Person Before the Law: the CAB Case for a Statement of Rights for People with Limited Leave in the UK*, NACAB, February 2000.

18.   UNHCR workshop, referenced in *Refugees' Reception and Settlement in Britain: A Report for the Joseph Rowntree Foundation*, Lynette Kelly and Danièle Joly, 20 April 1999.

19.   Refugee Council, *Refugee Resources in the UK*, Refugee Council, London, 1999.

20.   *Immigration and Asylum Act 1999*, The Stationary Office, 1999.

21.   Letter from Local Government Association (LGA) to regional consortia lead officers, 'Asylum seekers: provision of council accommodation', 2 February 2000.

22.   Correspondence from National Asylum Support Service to Audit Commission, 20 April 2000.

23.   Letter from LGA to NASS, 'Contract negotiations', 27 March 2000.

24.   Housing Corporation, *A Housing Plus Approach to Achieving Sustainable Communities*, Housing Corporation, 1997.

25.   Roger Zetter and Martyn Pearl, *Guidelines for Registered Social Landlords on the Provision of Housing and Support Services for Asylum Seekers*, Housing Corporation, November 1999.

26.   Refugee Council, *Rent-in-advance Guarantee Scheme: End of Project Report*, Refugee Council, March 1998.

27.   D Friedman and S Clohesy, *Housing Benefit System in Crisis*, National Housing Federation, October 1999.

28.   Correspondence from Benefits Agency to Audit Commission, 30 March 2000.

29.   See Legal Aid Board (LAB), *Reforming the Civil Advice and Assistance Scheme*, LAB, April 1998, for national breakdown of legal aid spending on immigration advice.

30.   A. Hayward, *Tuberculosis Control in London: The need for change – A report for the Thames Regional Directors of Public Health*, NHS Executive, 1998.

31.   D. Jones and P. Gill, 'Breaking down language barriers: The NHS needs to provide accessible interpreting services for all,' *British Medical Journal*, 316, 1998.

32.   S. Hargreaves, A. Holmes and J. Friedland, 'Health care provision for asylum seekers and refugees in the UK', *The Lancet*, 353, 1999.

33.   Department of Health (DoH), *Health Service Circular* (HSC) 1999/107: *Allocation of DDRB £60 million to GPs, Model Local Development Schemes*, DoH, April 1999.

34.   Mental Health Foundation, *Mental Healthcare for Refugees and Asylum Seekers: A Guide for Advisory Workers*, Mental Health Foundation, 1999.

35.   Information provided by the Department of Health, based on local authority grant claim returns.

36.   Data from Department of Health.

37.   Peabody Trust/ London Research Centre (LRC), *Refugee Skills-Net: The Employment and Training of Skilled and Qualified Refugees*, Peabody Trust/ LRC, June 1999.

38.   'Who wants to be a millionaire?' *The Independent Magazine*, 1 March 1997; see also Katharine Knox and Tony Kushner, *Refugees In An Age of Genocide*, Frank Cass, 1999 for further information on refugee contributions.

39.   Carey-Wood, Duke, Karn and Marshall, *Home Office Study 141; The Settlement of Refugees in Britain*, HMSO, London, 1995.

40.   Helga Pile, *The Asylum Trap: The Labour Market Experiences of Refugees with Professional Qualifications*, The Low Pay Unit, 1997.

41.   Home Office, 'A consultation paper on the integration of recognised refugees in the United Kingdom', third draft, Home Office, September 1999.

42.   Data supplied by the Home Office for single adults and families and from the Department of Health for unaccompanied minors.

43.   London Research Centre (LRC), *Refugees and Asylum Seekers in London: Financial Impact of Social Services and Housing Duties*, LRC, September 1998.

44.   *Local Government Finance (England): Special Grant Report No. 49*, laid before Parliament by the Home Secretary, Spring 2000.

45.   'Asylum Seeker Costs Model', prepared by the Home Office Research, Development and Statistics Directorate, Immigration Research and Statistics Service, 25 January 2000. A draft of the costing model is available on the internet at: http://www.homeoffice.gov.uk/rds/areas/immif.htm

Index References are to paragraph numbers, Boxes and Case Studies (page numbers)